HILTON CARTER

WILD
INTERIORS

HILTON CARTER

WILD
INTERIORS

BEAUTIFUL PLANTS IN BEAUTIFUL SPACES

CICO BOOKS

LONDON NEW YORK

Designer Megan Smith
Photographer Hilton Carter
Editor Anna Galkina
Art director Sally Powell
Production controller David Hearn
Publishing manager Penny Craig
Publisher Cindy Richards

Published in 2020 by CICO Books
An imprint of Ryland Peters
& Small Ltd
20–21 Jockey's Fields
London WC1R 4BW
and
341 E 116th St
New York, NY 10029

www.rylandpeters.com

10 9 8 7 6 5 4 3 2 1

A CIP catalog record for this book
is available from the Library of
Congress and the British Library.

ISBN: 978-1-78249-875-9

Printed in China

WINDOW DIRECTION AND LIGHT LEVELS
Understanding the types of light you
have in your home will make a big
difference to the choice of plants you
can place in those areas. Here's a
breakdown of the types of light your
plants will receive in the northern
hemisphere, depending on the
direction in which a window is facing
(these directions will be reversed if
you live in the southern hemisphere):

NORTHERN EXPOSURE Medium
to bright indirect light
NORTHEAST EXPOSURE Medium
to bright indirect light. Depending
on the time of year, direct sunlight
in the morning
NORTHWEST EXPOSURE Bright
indirect light
EASTERN EXPOSURE Direct morning
sunlight to bright indirect light
SOUTHERN EXPOSURE Bright indirect
light to medium light
SOUTHEAST EXPOSURE Bright
indirect light
SOUTHWEST EXPOSURE Bright
indirect light to direct afternoon
sunlight
WESTERN EXPOSURE Bright indirect
light to direct afternoon sunlight

CONTENTS

INTRODUCTION

Inside me, there's a deep need to surround myself with greenery. I go out of my way to try and make this a reality in every part of my life. Whether that's in the plant-filled environment I have created at home, the lushness of my studio, or searching for the local conservatory or botanical gardens in every town I visit. Something in me is just drawn to a place that's full of plants. You know that feeling you get when you look up and turn your face to the sun on the first warm day of spring? That feeling of warmth on your skin, the smell of the end of winter in the air, the smile on your face as you feel the first signs of spring—that's the feeling I get every time I enter a space with plants. These spaces give me life, and many others can relate to that. These spaces are what I like to call wild interiors. We are so fortunate to live in a time where, more than ever before, spaces like this are being created. Whether that's in homes, restaurants, hotels, or train stations, filling places where people gather with greenery has become a new way of life. To so many of us, this need to surround ourselves with plants is just that: life.

After the release of my first book, *Wild at Home*, I went on a book tour so I could meet people in the green-loving community. It was in these moments that the idea of creating a book titled *Wild Interiors* blossomed. Yes, prepare yourself for a few plant puns. And by "few" I mean many. During the tour, I got the chance to have personal conversations about plants and the care program a person will undertake to make their home an oasis. I quickly realized there were so many unique stories of how someone comes to bring plants into their home, discovering a true

passion they weren't aware of before. Because of these interactions, I wanted to hear more, see more, and meet some of the people who aren't just bringing plants into their homes for the sake of doing so, but with a real stylistic eye and reason. I wanted to see the different types of spaces people were working with. From the large spaces full of light, to the small, cave-like spaces with minimal light. This would become the backbone of what makes up *Wild Interiors*. So, I traveled to cities in Europe and the USA, met people creating lush spaces, and discussed their journeys in greenery with them. I wanted them to share their stories, challenges, and tips, and open a little window into their homes for the reader to see into, so they could possibly relate on some level. I knew some would feel inspired by these homes, but not know where to start or what plants to bring into their home, so providing a breakdown of what types of plants work best in certain rooms was important to me. I also found myself inspired by the plant shops, greenhouses, and commercial spaces in these cities. I saw how popular some plants were becoming in different parts of the world and which trendy plants will soon make their way into the spotlight. I felt that all the ideas I gathered on my travels were perfect to share here.

Overall, while I love the idea of *Wild Interiors* becoming a coffee table book, my goal was to see these places and hear these stories, so that the content here would inspire more people to bring plants into their home and into other spaces they want to make feel more alive. Because in doing so, every room can feel like the first warm day of spring.

INSPIRED

Where does one find inspiration? Is it found in the places we visit, the people we surround ourselves with, or the day-to-day things that permeate our lives? I think that's a resounding "yes, all of the above." For me, when it comes to bringing greenery into my home and finding ways to seamlessly style plants, I find myself finding inspiration in so many different places. Whether that's via social media, reading through books or magazines, watching style-heavy films, visiting amazing plant shops, or, probably my favorite pastime—going to botanical gardens and conservatories around the world. I've been inspired so deeply by what I've seen in these places. I take note of where they place their plants and how they create environments that are natural to those plants so they can live better lives. This really helps me understand how to work greenery into my home. I also use the time that I spend in these places to give myself a moment to take in a fresh breath, to hide away from the hustle and bustle of the streets, and place myself in a more tranquil environment. A few moments of mindfulness and self-care go a long way. In the following pages are a few places I've been to that are truly inspiring and could become a perfect way to start your day.

PLANT INSPIRATIONS

10 PLACES THAT HAVE INSPIRED ME

PLACE *Barbican Conservatory*
LOCATION *London, UK*

Brutalism is one of the architectural styles that has influenced me the most. I'm not sure how it started, but as a kid I remember loving the look and feel of all the buildings in the movie *Blade Runner*. That vision of a dystopian future just grabbed me. So, when I was in London and had the opportunity to visit the Barbican Centre's Conservatory, I didn't pass it up. You see, this beautiful place is only open on Sundays, so you have to hit it at the right time. For me, it was definitely right place, right time. In the Barbican Conservatory I found two of my favorite things: brutalist architecture and plants. There's something so appealing about the cold, hard, blocky concrete next to the delicate green foliage of the plants, not to mention my love of color palettes that mix grays and greens. Here, you're moving through a space that feels like what I'd imagine a shopping mall that has been abandoned for decades to feel like, one which houses over 2,000 plant species. Large *monsteras* and philodendrons climb the sides of indoor structures, while hundreds of other plant species cascade from the bridges and railings above. If this were my home, I'd never leave—I'm sure you can relate. Tucked away on the second level is a small desert room that has some of the most amazing cacti and succulents. I left the conservatory feeling refreshed, clear, and inspired. So much so, I designed my Rona planter with this place in mind.

PLACE *Rawlings Conservatory*
LOCATION *Baltimore, Maryland, USA*

The Rawlings Conservatory is one of my most inspiring places in Baltimore. As a kid growing up in the city, there wasn't much greenery around, unless you count weeds as greenery. The color palette here, as in most urban environments, is a mix of cement and brick, and if you're lucky, you'll get a touch of green. So, finding a little green in your day can be a bit difficult. Built in 1888 and located in the Druid Hill Park area of the city, the Rawlings Conservatory is the second largest conservatory in the USA. As a kid, I remember driving past the main greenhouse on our way to visit the Maryland Zoo and wondering exactly what was in this gorgeous building. Its shape and size were unlike any place I had seen in my life. Where I lived, homes were attached shoulder-to-shoulder. I don't recall ever going inside the greenhouse, but I often wonder how it would have affected me if I had.

I do know that I found my passion for greenery at the right moment for me. That flame would be ignited in the early part of 2014. When I moved back to Baltimore in 2015, I decided that I wanted to live in the city, but in a space surrounded by plant life, so I moved into an old mill apartment building along the Jones Falls River, which just so happens to be directly across from Druid Hill Park. So now, whenever I need to escape from the day to get a little fresh air, or just to feel a bit more inspired, I take a stroll over to the conservatory to get my fix. Inside, you'll find plants from all over the world—many that I probably would never see in person if they weren't all collected here. I do often see plants that I have in my own home, so I take the time to notice the type of environment they're in so that I can use that knowledge later. Today, while the city still isn't as lush as I would like it to be, that passion for greenery is deeply embedded in me and this place has helped in the process. I've never owned a home but, inspired by this place, I'm hoping to one day own a home with a greenhouse attached.

PLACE *Isabella Stewart Gardner Museum*
LOCATION *Boston, Massachusetts, USA*

If we're talking about inspiration let's not forget to acknowledge the efforts of Isabella Stewart Gardner. She did it right. She collected beautiful works of art, and when she didn't have enough room for them all in her home, she and her husband had a new building built. This place (or should I say, palace) was not just for them to enjoy, but for others to visit, too. That palace became the Isabella Stewart Gardner Museum, built in 1901. With all the beautiful art and architectural choices inside the museum, the place that inspired me most was the courtyard in the center of the building. And you can see why—built with a mixture of stone columns, pink stucco walls, and breathtaking archway windows, this four-story oasis is every indoor gardener's dream. It's what we all want—a greenhouse inside our home. Tree ferns, cacti, philodendrons, and many other plant species all call it home. It's such a beautiful sight to see. Of course, it takes a lot of money to create something like this, but that's where dreams and inspirations are conceived. While we might never have the money to build something like this in our own personal palaces, we can pull from what was done here to create something more realistic. At least that's my plan. Now, no trip to Boston is complete without a stop at this museum. Thanks Mrs. Gardner.

PLACE *Royal Botanic Gardens*
LOCATION *Kew, London, UK*

My wife, Fiona, and I took a trip to London in spring 2019, and it couldn't have been a more perfect time to visit. So many sights to see, but the one I needed to cross off my list was the Royal Botanic Gardens at Kew. This botanical garden was founded in the mid-eighteenth century, but it wasn't until 1848 when the Palm House—the place I found the most inspirational—was finally completed. To know me is to know how much of a sucker I am for a palm house, and the one at Kew does not disappoint. Before you even walk in, inspiration can be found in the exterior structure of the greenhouse. With its Victorian design and large scale, it's just breathtaking. What I found inspiring was the framing of the glass and, above all, the doorways. I mean, my God! They need to start bringing back structures like this—or at least build one for me. Once I was able to look past the beauty of the exterior, we entered the palm house, greeted by the sound of hissing mist and tropical greenery swaying in the light breeze from fans. Inside, you can see the beauty of the greenery against the white-painted steel frame of the greenhouse, not just from ground level, but from above, too, because of the gorgeous spiral staircases located at both ends. Every part of this greenhouse makes you wish you could move in, or at least stay the night. For me and Fiona, we're still trying to recreate the feeling we had there in our own home. Here's hoping.

5

PLACE *Garfield Park Conservatory*
LOCATION *Chicago, Illinois, USA*

Here in the US, when our professional sports teams win championship games, they always say they're going to Disney World. If it were me, I'd celebrate by going to Garfield Park Conservatory. If you've been there, I'm sure you'd understand what I mean, but if you haven't, what are you waiting for? The Garfield Park Conservatory was built in 1908 and was known to some as "landscape art under glass." It's pretty clear once you enter the front doors why it's referred to as that. Can you recall your first breath? That's the best way for me to describe what entering the conservatory for the first time felt like. Close your eyes, breathe in deeply, and slowly breathe out. This conservatory has the feeling we've all been trying to bottle and bring into our homes. What changed and inspired me the most was the fern room. I've been to many conservatories around the world, but have never experienced anything like it before. Time felt like it stopped completely. I was transported to a mystical world of beauty unfurling right before me. I'm sure the other visitors that saw me there thought I was a little out of my mind, because a smile was fixed on my face and the word "wow" kept floating from my mouth at every twist and turn in the room. I could say it was a whisper but, knowing myself, I'm sure it came out as "woooooooooooooow." The sheer scale of the room and the variety of ferns was just mind-blowing and mind-changing. Mind-changing

because I had never before been much of a fern-lover, but I definitely was when I left. And I didn't want to leave. I took every moment in, studying the plants, paying attention to the humidity in the air, the way staghorn ferns (*Platycerium* species) were suspended in the room, and so on. Mental notes became written notes, and those were supported by pictures, just in case my writing couldn't do it justice. As I write, I feel like I'm writing a love letter to the Garfield Park Conservatory and, more specifically, its fern room. I'm already married, but I feel like the next time I'm in Chicago I should write a little note that says: "Do you like me? Circle 'yes' or 'no'" and slip it under the door of the conservatory. Sorry Fiona, you'll always be my fern room in human form.

PLACE *1 Hotel Brooklyn Bridge*
LOCATION *Brooklyn, New York, USA*

This eco-friendly hotel is truly my home away from home. With greenery sprinkled throughout the lobby, a beautiful green wall in the living room, and plants in each room, this is what I want every place to look like when I am away from my own home.

PLACE *Shinjuku Gyoen National Garden*
LOCATION *Shinjuku City, Tokyo, Japan*

For me, every visit to Tokyo is as eye-opening as the first. With all the futuristic sensory overload the city has to offer, it's also full of places to escape and find some peace of mind. No place is better for this than the Shinjuku Gyoen National Garden. The conservatory is tranquil and lush, and the vast outdoor gardens are to die for when in full bloom.

PLACE *La Condesa*
LOCATION *Mexico City, Mexico*

Mexico City is like New York City, but with a lushness like no other urban city I've been to. While you probably won't find much indoor greenery here, it's the outdoor treatment that makes the city feel so vibrant and lush. Everywhere you turn, tropical plants emerge from the city floor.

PLACE *Conservatory of Flowers*
LOCATION *San Francisco, California, USA*

The beauty of this conservatory is seen both inside and out. I have found so much inspiration here for plant styling and for how I'd like to build a greenhouse for my dream home.

PLACE *Casa de las Olas*
LOCATION *Tulum, Mexico*

This place has so much magic to it. Specifically for my wife and I, this magic is embedded in the earth of the city. You see, Tulum inspired us so much we decided to get married there, and we even wrote our vows on biodegradable paper with wildflower seeds embedded within, which we buried deep in the soil of the city.

ON MY WISH LIST

1. Gardens by the Bay—*Singapore*
2. Jewel Changi Airport—*Singapore*
3. Madrid Atocha Railway Station—*Madrid, Spain*
4. Olympic National Park—*Washington, USA*
5. Royal Greenhouses of Laeken—*Brussels, Belgium*
6. Spiral Treetop Walkway—*Copenhagen, Denmark*

PLANT ENVY

THE NEXT 10 "IT" PLANTS

When I started my plant journey back in 2014, the first plant I bought was a fiddle-feaf fig (*Ficus lyrata*). They were all the rage then and were the interior designer's plant of choice —they were definitely the "it" plant. They appeared in magazine articles, movies, and TV shows. For a plant newbie, it placed me at the level of the tastemakers. OK, maybe not, but when friends came over, though they didn't know what kind of plant it was, they did know it was a very cool plant. A couple of years passed, and the fiddle hype made way for the *Monstera* hype. And after that, the *Pilea* hype, then back to the fiddle. I loved the attention the fiddle-leaf fig got. I started with one and now have four, and they all have names: Frank, Treezus, Li'l baby, and Clavel. One of the good things that happens when a plant becomes popular is that the price goes down. It used to be difficult to find fiddle-leaf figs, but now you can find them in hardware stores and sometimes even grocery stores. What's less good about their popularity is that you're no longer as cool as you

thought. No, you're cool, we all are. Now, you can level up your coolness by getting what I believe will be the "nexy" plants. Yeah, "nexy" is what happens when "next" and "sexy" have a baby. See, you're all getting cooler by the minute.

NOTE The window directions and light levels mentioned here refer to those living in the northern hemisphere. These directions will be reversed if you live in the southern hemisphere. See note on page 4.

WATERMELON BEGONIA
(PEPEROMIA ARGYREIA)

I love watermelon. I can't think of anyone that doesn't. I almost feel the same way about the watermelon begonia, but not quite, because it doesn't grow little watermelons as you think it would—instead, the name is based on the colors and shape of the foliage. It grows in a compact shape, so you won't have to worry about the watermelon begonia taking up too much space. Mixed in with your other plants, the watermelon begonia looks so unique that it will be a stand-out.

LIGHT For the best growth and to keep the foliage vibrant, find a spot that has bright indirect to medium light. The brighter, the better, but a mix of dappled light throughout the day will work well. Avoid exposure to direct sun, which will burn the leaf tissue, leaving your peperomia with brown spots. For balanced growth, rotate every three to four weeks.

TEMPERATURE Keep this plant in a nice warm spot, between 65–80°F (18–27°C) during the day and no colder than 60°F (15°C) at night. Keep away from the direct blast of air conditioners and heaters.

WATER Give your peperomia a drink when the top 2 in (5 cm) of soil is dry. Plant it in a pot that has a drainage hole and make sure to water until the excess water comes out into the base tray. Discard the excess water, as leaving your plant sitting in water will lead to root rot and kill it over time. Under-watering will eventually curl the peperomia's leaves and turn its tips brown and, again, lead to death.

REPOTTING Repot during the growing season in spring or summer. A good indicator that it's time for a new pot is when you notice the roots of the plant creeping out of the drainage hole of the pot. Make sure the new pot is at least 2 in (5 cm) larger than the previous pot. When it's time to repot, try to do so on the day you intend to water it. A plant with dry soil is easier to repot than one with wet soil.

2 CROCODILE FERN
(*MICROSORUM MUSIFOLIUM* 'CROCODYLLUS')

A rose by any other name... I mean, what else were they supposed to call this insanely cool fern other than "Crocodile." Nature is amazing, right? The foliage of the crocodile fern is as sleek and smooth as the reptile itself, but please don't try making boots with it! With the ability to grow to about 5 ft (1.5 m) in its natural habitat, your indoor fern will grow wild if it has the right light and care.

LIGHT Look for a spot that gets bright indirect to low light. If you have a northeast-facing window, place your crocodile fern somewhere close to it. Like all ferns, avoid exposure to direct sun, which will burn the leaf tissue, leaving your fern with crispy brown edges and eventually killing it. For balanced growth, rotate every three to four weeks.

TEMPERATURE Remember that this is a tropical plant, so keeping it in a nice warm spot is best, between 65–80°F (18–27°C) during the day and no colder than 60°F (15°C) at night. Keep this fern away from the direct blast of air conditioners and heaters.

WATER Unlike most ferns, you should only water the crocodile fern when the top 1–2 in (2.5–5 cm) of soil is somewhat dry. Plant in a pot that has a drainage hole and make sure to water until the excess water comes out into the base tray. Discard the excess water, as leaving your plant sitting in water will lead to root rot and kill it over time. Under-watering will eventually curl the crocodile fern's leaves and turn its tips brown and, again, lead to death. Mist the leaves weekly if your home is dry.

REPOTTING Repot during the growing season in spring or summer. A good indicator that it's time for a new pot is when you notice the roots of the plant creeping out of the drainage hole of the pot. Make sure the new pot is at least 2 in (5 cm) larger than the previous pot.

CALATHEA ORBIFOLIA

I have so much love for tropical plants, and this beauty shows off every reason why. Native to Bolivia, it has beautiful, ping pong paddle-shaped foliage in bold pale green and dark green stripes, so this *calathea* instantly stands out from the crowd. While it isn't for every home, when placed in the right environment it can grow fairly large, becoming an instant "statement plant."

LIGHT To keep the foliage vibrant, you have to place it in the right light. The perfect spot is one that has medium light. Avoid exposure to direct sun, which will burn the leaf tissue, leaving your plant with brown spots. For balanced growth, rotate every three to four weeks.

TEMPERATURE Cool and calm is the mood of this *calathea*, but not too cold. The ideal temperature is 65–80°F (18–27°C) during the day and no colder than 60°F (15°C) at night. Keep away from the direct blast of air conditioners and heaters.

WATER Just like most *calatheas*, *Calathea orbifolia* will need its soil to stay evenly moist, so it should be watered more often. This does not mean drowning it in a pot with little or no drainage, as overwhelming the roots with too much water will strip away the vibrant color, fading the foliage. Under-watering this plant will eventually curl leaves and turn their tips brown, leading to death. Mist the leaves weekly if your home is dry.

REPOTTING Repot during the growing season in spring or summer. A good indicator that it's time for a new pot is when you notice the roots of the plant creeping out of the drainage hole of the pot. Make sure the new pot is at least 2 in (5 cm) larger than the previous pot. When it's time to repot, it's a good idea to do so on the day you intend to water it. A plant with dry soil is easier to repot than one with wet soil.

FAN PALM
(LICUALA GRANDIS)

Out of all the plants in this list, I believe the *Licuala* will be the most sought-after plant in the years to come. I mean, look at it! They can grow up to 5–6 ft (1.5–1.8 m), so you might want to place them in a spot where they can truly express themselves.

LIGHT For the best growth, this plant will need bright indirect light. The brighter, the better, but dappled light throughout the day will work well—a sunny window would be ideal. Avoid exposure to direct sun, which will burn the leaf tissue, leaving your *Licuala* with brown spots. For balanced growth, rotate every three to four weeks.

TEMPERATURE Think tropical and find a warm spot in your home between 65–80°F (18–27°C), and do not let it get close to the colder end of that 65°F (18°C). Keeping it at 74°F (23°C) would be perfect. Keep away from the direct blast of air conditioners and heaters.

WATER The *Licuala* will need its soil to stay evenly moist. In order to stay on top of this, take your finger and stick it into the soil at least 1 in (2.5 cm) down. If your finger comes out with soil on it, it's moist enough, and you can wait a few days before you test it again. If it comes out dry, it's time to water. Overwatering your plant can lead to the foliage turning yellow, and possibly root rot. You'll need to water less in the colder months, but always use your finger to get a good sense of the moisture level. Mist the leaves weekly if your home is dry.

REPOTTING Repot during the growing season in spring or summer. A good indicator that it's time for a new pot is when you notice the roots of the plant creeping out of the drainage hole of the pot. Make sure the new pot is at least 2 in (5 cm) larger than the previous pot. When it's time to repot, it's a good idea to do so on the day you intend to water it. A plant with dry soil is easier to repot than one with wet soil.

BANYAN
(FICUS BENGHALENSIS 'AUDREY')

Move over fiddle-leaf fig. Here comes the ficus everyone will be talking about. It can grow to about 20 ft (6 m) in the wild, so in your home, the beauty of this plant will make a real statement. And that statement would be: you have a tree in your house. While it probably won't grow as tall indoors as in the wild, you'll want to leave room for it to stretch out its arms.

LIGHT For the best growth, this plant needs to be in bright indirect light. Dappled light throughout the day will work well—a sunny

window would be ideal. Direct sun is to be avoided, so being near west-facing windows is not good for this plant. Afternoon direct sun can burn the leaf tissue, creating yellow and brown spots. For balanced growth, rotate every three to four weeks.

TEMPERATURE Between 65–80°F (18–27°C) during the day and no colder than 60°F (15°C) at night. Your goal is to mimic its natural habitat as closely as you can.

WATER The rule of thumb for ficus and most other tropical plants is to only water when the top 2 in (5 cm) of soil is completely dry. To test for this, stick your finger into the soil at least 1 in (2.5 cm) down. If your finger comes out with soil on it, wait a few days before you test it again. Planters with drainage holes are best. Make sure to water it until the excess water runs out into the base tray. Discard excess water, as leaving your plant sitting in water will lead to root rot and kill your plant over time. Mist the leaves weekly if your home is dry.

REPOTTING Repot during spring or summer. A good indicator that it's time for a new pot is when you notice the roots of the plant creeping out of the drainage hole of the pot. Make sure the new pot is at least 2 in (5 cm) larger than the previous pot.

6

MONSTROSE APPLE CACTUS
(*CEREUS PERUVIANUS* 'MONSTROSUS')

While many people have standard cacti in their homes, why not get a little wild and bring in a twisted monstrose apple cactus instead? I think if I could start all over again, I'd fill my home with nothing but cacti. If you put them in front of your windows, they make for great home security, plus you'd have more free time because you wouldn't have to water your plants as often. What's great about the monstrose apple cactus is that while it is a cactus, its spines aren't too long, making it a more friendly cactus to have in a living space. With its twisted shape, it looks like a cactus in a Salvador Dalí painting.

LIGHT For the best growth, this cactus needs to be in bright indirect to full morning sun. The brighter, the better, but a south/southeast-facing window would be ideal. While morning sun will be ok, afternoon direct sun would be a problem and could burn your cactus. For balanced growth, rotate every three to four weeks.

TEMPERATURE Keep your cacti in a warm place in your home, between 60–85°F (16–29°C)

during the day and no colder than 55°F (13°C) at night.

WATER Only water when the soil is completely dry. I water once every three weeks during the warmer months and every four to six months during the colder months. A terracotta or ceramic pot that has a drainage hole is perfect for a cactus, because letting it sit in a pot without drainage is an easy way to overwater. The rule of thumb here is that you'll be better off under-watering than overwatering. Think about the deserts they live in.

REPOTTING Repot during spring or summer. A good indicator that it's time for a new pot is when you notice the roots of the plant creeping out of the drainage hole of the pot. Make sure the new pot is at least 2 in (5 cm) larger than the previous pot.

7 BURRO'S TAIL
(*SEDUM MORGANIANUM*)

Looking for a beautiful trailing plant for a hanging planter? The Mexican burro's tail is ideal, as they can cascade down 6 ft (1.8 m) or more. With clusters of pellet-like leaves, they're beautiful plants to have indoors, especially during spring and summer when they can grow small pink flowers —but only with the right care and in the right light. Quick note: the string-of-pearls (*Senecio rowleyanus*) also has similar needs if you like this plant.

LIGHT For the best growth, the plant needs to be in bright indirect light. The brighter, the better, but dappled light throughout the day will work well—a sunny window would be ideal. While morning sun will be ok, afternoon direct sun will be a problem, as it will burn the leaf tissue, leaving the foliage dry and prune-like. For balanced growth, rotate every three to four weeks.

TEMPERATURE Keep the plant in a warm spot, between 65–80°F (18–27°C) during the day and no colder than 60°F (15°C) at night. Mimic the plant's natural habitat as closely as you can.

WATER I only water my burro's tail when the soil is completely dry, which normally works out as once every two weeks. Planting a burro's tail in a pot that has a drainage hole is key, because letting it sit in a pot without drainage is an easy way to overwater. If the leaves start to turn yellowish in color, you'll know it's having too much water. An indication that it's ready for water is if the leaves look a little wrinkly. The rule of thumb here is that you'll be better off under-watering the burro's tail than you will be in giving it a drink when it's not thirsty. Most plants are killed because of overwatering rather than under-watering. Remember that.

REPOTTING Try to repot during the growing season in spring and summer. However, the burro's tail likes a smaller pot, so you won't be repotting it very often. It's a good idea to do this on the day you intend to water it. A plant with dry soil is easier to repot than one with wet soil. The leaves of a burro's tail are really fragile and break off easily, so be gentle and take your time when repotting.

COUNCIL TREE
(FICUS ALTISSIMA)

I can't get enough of a good ficus, and the *Ficus altissima* is just so, so good. When I first laid eyes on it at a nursery in Baltimore, I thought it was some sort of rubber plant because of the shape and colors of its leaves, which are a mix of lime- and fern-green. This tropical plant can grow up to 60 ft (18 m) in the wild, but don't count on that happening in your home—well, not unless you live in a greenhouse, and if that's the case, when can I move in? What I love about this ficus is that it's not as fussy as its cousin the fiddle-leaf fig, and it will look great nestled next to any other plant you have in your collection. If you're looking to really bring life and color to a room, the *Ficus altissima* is the perfect plant baby.

LIGHT Treat *Ficus altissima* as you would other ficus plants. For the best growth, it needs to be in bright indirect light. The brighter, the better, but a mix of dappled light throughout the day will work well. A sunny window would be ideal. Direct sun is to be avoided, so being near west-facing windows is not good for this plant. While morning sun directly kissing the leaves will be ok, it's afternoon direct sun that will be a problem.

It will burn the leaf tissue, leaving the foliage with yellowish and brown spots that look different to the brown tips you get from under-watering. For balanced growth, rotate every three to four weeks.

TEMPERATURE Keep your *Ficus altissima* in a nice warm spot in your home, between 65–80°F (18–27°C) during the day and no colder than 60°F (15°C) at night. Your goal is to mimic its natural habitat as closely as you can.

WATER The rule of thumb for ficus and most other tropical plants is to only water when the top 2 in (5 cm) of soil is completely dry. To test for this, take your finger and stick it into the soil at least 1 in (2.5 cm) down. If your finger comes out with soil on it, you can wait a few days before you test it again. Plant it in a pot that has a drainage hole and make sure to water until the excess water comes out into the base tray. Discard the excess water, as leaving your plant sitting in water will lead to root rot and kill it over time. Under-watering will eventually turn the tips brown and, again, lead to death. Mist the leaves weekly if your home is dry.

REPOTTING Repot during spring or summer. A good indicator that it's time for a new pot is when you notice the roots of the plant creeping out of the drainage hole of the pot. Make sure the new pot is at least 2 in (5 cm) larger than the previous pot. When it's time to repot, it's a good idea to do this on the day you intend to water it. A plant with dry soil is easier to repot than one with wet soil.

FABIAN ARALIA
(POLYSCIAS 'FABIAN')

Like most children in the US, I grew up reading the books of Dr. Seuss. If I had to pick a favorite, I'd have to go with *Green Eggs and Ham*. The stories are so fun and the illustrations so wild and dreamlike. One of the things that stuck with me was the shape and design of the trees. The Fabian aralia reminds me of something out of one of Dr. Seuss's books. Its beauty and weirdness comes from its thick, burly trunk from which sprout thin, speckled branches that produce pancake-shaped foliage which is dark green on top and violet on the bottom. The sculptural shape of this aralia makes it perfect for a home that is looking to stand out.

LIGHT For the best growth, this aralia needs to be in bright indirect light. The brighter, the better—a mix of dappled light throughout the day will work well. A sunny window would be ideal. Direct sun is to be avoided, so being near west-facing windows is not good for this plant. While morning sun will be ok, afternoon direct sun will be a problem, burning the leaf tissue, and leaving the foliage with yellowish and brown spots. For balanced growth, rotate every three to four weeks.

TEMPERATURE The Fabian aralia needs to be in a warm spot in your home, between 65–80°F (18–27°C) during the day and no colder than 60°F (15°C) at night. Finding a space that's close to the mid-70s (about 24°C) would be ideal.

WATER You should water only when the top 2 in (5 cm) of soil is completely dry. To test for this, take your finger and stick it into the soil at least 1 in (2.5 cm) down. If your finger comes out with soil on it, you can wait a few days before you test it again. Plant it in a pot that has a drainage hole and make sure to water until the excess water comes out into the base tray. Discard the excess water, as leaving your plant sitting in water will lead to root rot and kill it over time. Under-watering will eventually turn the tips brown and, again, lead to death, but it will tolerate being under-watered more often than being overwatered.

REPOTTING Repot during spring or summer. A good indicator that it's time for a new pot is when you notice the roots of the plant creeping out of the drainage hole of the pot. Make sure the new pot is at least 2 in (5 cm) larger than the previous pot.

10

MEXICAN TREE FERN
(CIBOTIUM SCHIEDEI)

I've always been in awe of the beauty of tree ferns. They aren't something you typically see in your local nursery, but, if you do, grab one. I always feel excited to watch ferns slowly unfurl their delicate new fronds. Unlike other ferns, tree ferns can grow up to 10 ft (3 m) in the wild. In your home, while it might start off on the smaller side, this gorgeous plant will make a real statement.

LIGHT Bright indirect to medium light works best. If you have northeast-facing windows or even eastern-facing windows that get dappled light, place your Mexican tree fern somewhere close to them. As with all ferns, do your best to avoid exposing this plant to direct sun, which will burn the leaf tissue, leaving your fern with crispy brown edges, eventually killing it. For balanced growth, rotate every three to four weeks.

TEMPERATURE Remember that this is a tropical plant, so keeping it in a warm place would be best, somewhere between 65–80°F (18–27°C) during the day and no colder than 60°F (15°C) at night. Keep away from the direct blasts of air conditioners and heaters.

WATER As with most ferns, you will need to keep the soil evenly moist. Never let the soil dry out completely—this doesn't mean drowning it in a pot with no drainage, because you will overwater the roots and the foliage will turn yellow. You'll need to water less in the colder months, but always use your finger to get a good sense of the moisture level. Mist the leaves weekly if your home is dry, or introduce a humidifier to the rooms where you have your ferns.

REPOTTING Repot during spring or summer. A good indicator that it's time for a new pot is when you notice the roots of the plant creeping out of the drainage hole of the pot. Make sure the new pot is at least 2 in (5 cm) larger than the previous pot.

JOURNEYS
IN GREENERY

When I was at film school, they taught us that when you're creating a character, you should always know that character's backstory. In comic books, it's known as the origin story. My own origin story, or I should say my "journey in greenery," began with a passion for creating spaces that tell a story about the characters that dwell within them. Working as a freelance director, I started paying more attention to the production design and the importance of making sure every detail in a scene spoke of who the character was. This made me start thinking about my own space and what the items and details there said about me. After that, the pieces I brought in would be forever pieces, things that had a story or would become a part of my story. With that, I started to bring in more plants. I understood how different I felt when the environments I was in had greenery, and knew I needed to have that same feeling in my home. Needless to say, of course one begets two and two begets hundreds. Now it wasn't that extreme, but I was, in a way, bitten by the bug. The power that plant life has in a home is transformative.

It's that same power that has so many people bringing greenery into their homes today. We are all part of a group I call "the plant-loving community." I had the wonderful opportunity to travel around the world and meet some of the individuals creating their own green-filled spaces, and they shared their origin stories with me. So sit back, take a journey with me, and see how the power of greenery has transformed these homes. Because, at the end of the day, some of us are Superman, born with the power, while some of us are Spiderman and were just bitten by the bug.

ABSTRACTS & GREENSCAPES

HOME *Alina Fassakhova*
LOCATION *Brooklyn, New York, USA*

You want to get wild? Let's get WILD! Not "take your shirt off and twirl it around your head like a helicopter" wild, but wild like "plant-crazy" wild. At least that's how I felt when I entered the home jungle of wonderfully talented painter, Alina Fassakhova. The jungle in question is a 1,000 ft² (93 m²) Brooklyn apartment that she shares with her husband Artem, her two cats, Usha and Sofie, and her 80 or so plants. When I think of New York apartments I picture spaces with small windows that face other large buildings, but this is certainly not that. "I was looking for an open-plan loft space filled with light, where I could live and work. This apartment was a perfect match," Alina says. I think the key words here are "filled with light"—the perfect conditions for her many beautiful plants to thrive.

"I CANNOT IMAGINE MY HOME WITHOUT PLANTS.
IT WOULD FEEL EMPTY AND LIFELESS. ESPECIALLY
WHEN YOU LIVE IN A BIG, BUSY CITY LIKE NEW YORK."

As Alina opened the door to her home, greeting me with a smile that a friend who hasn't seen you in a while would, I was instantly aware of the light that comes flooding into her home. Along the far wall of her apartment, running the entire length of it, in fact, were beautiful large windows. And unlike most apartments in the city, her windows faced out to a wide open sky. A southwest-facing sky to be exact—perfect for giving many types of plants the levels of light they need to thrive. Once you get past how large the windows are and the view outside, the next thing you notice is how at home you feel right away. When I asked Alina how she'd describe her interior style, she answered: "Eclectic—I like to mix and match vintage items, objects I bought on my travels, flea market finds, and modern furniture to create visual texture that makes the loft look cozy and inviting. In addition, this space is all about tropical plants coexisting with contemporary art, because I use it as my studio." This is clear for sure. Woven into the greenery that grows from every corner of the apartment, you'll find Alina's works of art, either finished or in progress. Sidenote: you'll also notice that Alina did the painting for the cover of this very book. Now that's WILD!

Alina's plant game is undeniably strong and her love for rare and challenging plants is clear. Walking through her home, you'll find variegated *Monstera* mixed with *Alocasia* and watermelon begonia (*Peperomia argyreia*). These are plants that aren't easy to care for,

but Alina's efforts and the light levels in her home make it all possible. "I've had plants in my apartments for as long as I can remember, but I had to leave all my plants back in Moscow when I moved to New York City in 2017. I started my current collection two years ago. Plants inspire me and give my eyes rest after hours of painting. For me, caring for plants can be a great form of mindfulness meditation. Over the years it has become a daily practice, and I try to dedicate at least an hour every day to spend with my plants." I couldn't agree with this more. This is the sort of dedication that is necessary when caring for green life. Finding her love for plants through the passion her mom and grandma had for greenery, Alina would find joy in reading plant care books as a child. It's in her DNA, maybe. Can green thumbs be handed down or is it something you acquire after many years of hard work? I'd say it's more the latter.

Understanding your space and the light in each room, for many people, dictates where one can place a plant. But for Alina, she is lucky, as most of her apartment is in bright light. When I asked her how she decides which rooms she'll place her plants in she said, "It all depends on the light and humidity requirements for each plant. For instance, full-sun plants get spots right by the windowsill, while my high-humidity tropicals get clustered together slightly away from the windows. I usually start by finding a spot where a plant would be happy." I think we all just want a nice spot in the sun and to find our happiness!

HEIGHT AND TEXTURE

Alina's studio apartment is a lesson in how open-plan living can optimize available space for displaying plants. Using shelves for trailing plants like *Stephania erecta* (above) and side tables for dramatic foliage, such as the spiny slender leaves of a chestnut dioon (*Dioon edule*), creates visual interest and can be fitted into small corners and empty walls. Opposite, Alina's workspace is screened from her bedroom area by the large leaves of a peace lily (*Spathiphyllum wallisii*).

GREENERY GALLERY
Alina's favorite corner of her home, where a thriving *Monstera adansonii* ranges up the wall above a beautiful *Philodendron pastazanum*. Alina's gorgeous paintings make for an ever-evolving art display, beautifully in tune with the greenery.

CREATIVE CONTAINERS

Hanging planters (top) are perfect if you have limited floor space—plus, they're a great way to keep plants out of reach of curious pets. Varieties of *Hoya carnosa* ('Chelsea', 'Compacta', and 'Variegata' are seen here) are ideal for hanging.

I think it's in plants that Alina finds her happiness. "I especially like the right corner of the living room, where the large *Philodendron pastazanum* spreads its enormous leaves and the mature *Monstera adansonii* climbs the wall above it vigorously. This gives me a very jungly feeling every time I sit on the couch and see that view," says Alina. I found her way of creating living screens to separate one part of the space from another very smart, whether it was the palms and large peace lily (*Spathiphyllum wallisii*) that separate her workspace from her bedroom, or the Alocasia and philodendrons that separate the living room from the kitchen. In an open floor plan, finding ways to seamlessly create partitions can be difficult. She has managed to make it feel natural and beautiful.

While Alina doesn't find it important to name her plants, when pressed to answer which of the 80 plants is her favorite, she replied, "It's very hard to pick a favorite one. They are all pretty special to me. But if I had to choose, I'd say the variegated *Monstera*, because every leaf has a unique abstract pattern. It's like a little surprise when a new leaf unfurls, because you never know what it is going to look like." I found her answer to this question pretty amazing, given that I feel the same way about her abstract paintings. When you look at the color pattern of a variegated leaf and then at one of her artworks, they feel very closely related.

BOTANICAL KITCHEN
Philodendron and Alocasia are used to separate Alina's kitchen from the rest of her living space, making the transition feel natural and not blocking out light like a solid screen would.

When it comes to her cats and the plants, she doesn't have many concerns. "Usha and Sofie love being surrounded with plants. I think they are used to them and consider themselves jungle cats. We've never had accidents with them nibbling on toxic plants. They like to play hide and seek among the leaves." Knowing what plants are toxic to your pets is important (see *Pets vs. Plants*, on page 210). Learning as you go is also important. When I asked Alina for one thing she's learned in her journey in greenery that could help others, she responded, "I like to read about a plant online before getting it. I personally pay attention to a plant's natural habitat (what country a plant is native to, the elevation it grows at in the wild, UV index, humidity, etc.). Based on that information, I try to recreate the best conditions for a plant to grow in my apartment. Another important recommendation is to spend time with your plants—to be observant, notice small changes. This helps you slowly figure out what a plant needs and likes." Bravo, Alina. Bravo.

> "I USUALLY START BY FINDING A SPOT WHERE
> A PLANT WOULD BE HAPPY."

RESTFUL BEDROOM

Growing plants over mirrors, as Alina has above her bed (opposite and above) is a great way to bounce light around, helping all the plants in a room— genius! Choose climbers like *Epipremnum pinnatum* 'Cebu Blue,' and let your eyes linger over the leaves as you drift off to sleep.

THE OLD BRAND NEW

HOME *Dabito*
LOCATION *Los Angeles, California, USA*

The first time I recall stumbling upon the beautiful work of the creative Dabito was back in 2015 when I was living in New Orleans and shopping for a new kitchen table. He had been featured on a blog I was skimming through, looking for inspiration for my new apartment. What instantly grabbed my attention was his use of color and how it beamed its way from my laptop screen and directly into my retinas. This need to surround himself with bold, bright colors was ever-present when I paid him a visit in the summer of 2019. Residing in Los Angeles, Dabito owns this 1,500 ft² (140 m²), mid-century home with his fiancé Ryan, their pups, Luigi and Sterling, and cat Verbena. The home they share is the true definition of eclectic. So many wonderful pops of color, pattern, and adventure.

You can feel the sense of exploration throughout Dabito and Ryan's home, as though you're on a guided tour of their travels. Each room has a good balance of old and new, textures on textures, and color theory. There's something rich and satisfying about each setup. "My style is a little bit modern and bohemian, collected and eclectic. I love using bold color, plants, art, and patterns to define spaces. I started out as a graphic designer, printmaker, and photographer. And even in my personal works, I've always used a lot of color. And once I was living on my own, I just filled my home with more color. I treat my home like a canvas. I think having a curious eye helps inspire how I style my home. Also traveling—even just to the flea market—can give you so many fun ideas!" says Dabito about his style and work. But honestly, he could just let it all speak for itself.

While the home has many natural touches, what I found interesting was how and when he decided to use greenery. Dabito says they have a total of 20 plants, but it feels like so much more. Maybe that's because in three of the rooms, he goes by my method of having a "statement plant" to set it off. The living room is led by a large banyan, *Ficus benghalensis* 'Audrey', the dining room by a large fiddle-leaf fig (*Ficus lyrata*), and the master bathroom by a large dragon tree (*Dracaena draco*). Dabito finds the perfect moments in his home to add a splash of living green, which never feel random. Although Dabito didn't grow up with plants in his home, he says "My family had an edible garden. We planted lots of fruit trees like guava, avocado, and pomegranate. We also had vegetables like squashes, bitter melons, and pennywort. I remember my senior year of high school, I finally got my own room, which was basically our living room—I come from an immigrant family so we were packed into a small house. And I remember seeing lots of plants in IKEA catalogs. I didn't have money or a car, so I would go into our yard and clip plants like snake plants and put them in vases. And when we were at the grocery store, I would beg my mom to buy a small plant for our bathroom. I guess that's how I got started with plants. I also worked for a vertical gardening company in my twenties and that spearheaded my love for plants." You can see this love spread around his home. But deciding how to spread that love isn't always easy; you can't just toss any kind of plant anywhere and call it a day. There has to be some intention behind each decision. Dabito comments, "I would say that I look for shape and color and also how much care they need." A designer's eye and a love of greenery can be a winning combination. Here, it's a glass slipper on the foot of Cinderella... the perfect fit. Ok, ok, that was a bit cheesy but I mean, come on! The placement of the *Ficus* is spot on.

Adding plants to a home can make a hard corner soft and bring life where there wasn't any before. It's that added bit of life that Dabito feels is necessary: "Plants are a really affordable way to personalize and fill a space. For me, they bring joy. I work from home and it can be lonely, and I feel like plants are just good company— they honestly make me feel less alone. So I have to have some sort of plant in each room or else it just feels really sterile and lifeless."

PLAYFUL COLOR

The plants in Dabito's living room are carefully chosen and work perfectly with his art, textiles, and furniture. All in stylish containers: an air plant (*Tillandsia*) in a little hammock hangs on the wall, a Swiss cheese plant (*Monstera deliciosa*) in a standing pot, and a staghorn fern (*Platycerium*) in a hand-painted pot sits on the sideboard.

"PLANTS ARE AN AFFORDABLE WAY TO MAKE
A SPACE FEEL MORE WARM AND WELCOMING,
ESPECIALLY FOR REALLY SMALL SPACES."

TOUCHES OF DRAMA

Above, the wavy leaves of a bird's-nest fern
(*Asplenium nidus*) work well with the linear tiles,
while on the left, Dabito's cat Verbena sweetly
rubs her cheek along a *Monstera deliciosa* leaf.
Opposite, an expressive fiddle-leaf fig (*Ficus lyrata*)
sets off an abstract print beautifully. The motion of
the brushstrokes mimics the shape and growth of the
foliage. On the table, a *Dracaena fragans* 'Warneckii'
looks unexpected in an orange bowl with pale stones.

I'm sure we all can agree with that. I find myself talking to my fiddle-leaf fig, Frank, often. But wait, Dabito also has his pets to keep him company while he works at home. When I asked how they get along with the plants, he replied, "Both Verbena and Luigi occasionally like to put their paws in the soil and dig a bit. For the most part, they leave the plants alone. Thank goodness! Verbena actually likes to brush her cheeks against their leaves. It's cute!"

While Dabito says his favorite kinds of plants have always been *Dracaena* and ferns, he couldn't pick a favorite plant from his collection. I can relate. Luckily, I did get Dabito to share a little helpful tip for how to go about shopping for a new plant: "Plants are an affordable way to make a space feel more warm and welcoming, especially for really small spaces. I've actually started to buy bigger plants with more established root systems. They don't dry out as fast as small potted plants. I'm not the best at watering sometimes. Some people overwater, I definitely under-water, so there's that." Self-awareness is one of the first steps in becoming a better plant parent. Dab, you're on it, my friend!

ARCHED AND LOVELY
I think the arched doorways in Dabito's home frame the views into the rooms beyond beautifully. The master bathroom, seen through the door, is home to a large "statement" dragon tree (*Dracaena draco*)—there's a closer view in the photo opposite).

MUTED BLOOMS

HOME *Theodora Melnik*
LOCATION *Berlin, Germany*

In the city of Berlin, nestled in a second-floor apartment, is where I found Theodora. To her friends she is just Theo, and that's what she asked me to call her. Plant friends unite! Theo lives in an "Altbau-" style flat in Neukölln, which was built around the turn of the 19th century and is characterized by its high ceilings, wooden floors, and stucco. These are the bones of the space, but it's in Theo's vision and creativity that the home (which she shares with her boyfriend Benjamin, her two cats, Charly and Miro, and her 150 plants) really comes alive. "I like to mix everything together. There's a bit mid-century, a touch of Bauhaus, some new pieces, and some over 100 years old. I always get new ideas and the result of that is the flat," says Theo.

"I FEEL THAT THE PLANT CRAZE AT THE MOMENT SEEMS
TO BE TOUCHING PEOPLE ON A DEEPER LEVEL, SO I'M
HOPEFUL THAT IT WILL ENDURE FOR A LONG TIME—
LONGER THAN A TREND CYCLE, THAT'S FOR SURE!"

When I entered Theo's flat, I was struck by the moody colors—those of you that know me might know my fondness for darker/moodier interiors. Well ,Theo's place and I spoke what some might call a "love language" with each other. The palette of the space was muted, allowing for the subtle pops of color to ring out (I'm speaking directly to her green velvet couch here). I found myself being taken aback by the details of the flat: the way the walls softly transition to become the ceiling, the beautiful ceiling molding that frames the light fixtures which cascade down in each room— so many wonderful touches! This all made me understand why Theo and Benjamin have been renting here for six years.

When I asked Theo if her day job inspires how she goes about her interior style, she replied, "I'm a copywriter, so it doesn't really have much to do with the way I style the home. But as a copywriter, I've noticed that advertising really works on me, and that is true for the flat as well. Often, though, I'll see something new that I want and know it was inspired by something old, and then I go looking for the old original instead." It's the mix of old and new that makes her place feel so warm and cozy, but it's in her plant styling that I truly feel at home. And in a flat that is only 667 ft² (62 m²), it's hard not to notice 150 plants. When I brought up how long she had been bringing plants into her living spaces, she said, "For a long time. My oldest plant I took from my parents home with me when I moved out. I've been caring for it for

over 15 years. I have always loved plants and flowers. My parents tell me it's been this way since I was a toddler." Having plants in the home as a kid really had a huge impact on Theo, and this is clear in her adulthood. You can still see a mix of childlike joys woven into her home. The best example of this is her bookshelf in the living room. You can learn a lot about an individual from their bookshelf and the way they style it. On Theo's bookshelf, you'll find a Bambi statuette mixed with small plants, terrariums, and other unique treasures, all interspersed with a selection of books coordinated by color. Below the shelves sits a vintage piano that doubles as a plant stand. This is next-level playing music for your plants; if it was me, I'd just put on some Bach and call it a day, but Theo plays the music herself. I'm kidding, I'm kidding. I'd never play Bach to my plants; we're more of a Beethoven kind of family. When I asked Theo which room was her favorite, she told me it was her kitchen, and that she really loved the botanical shelf in there— who doesn't love a good plant shelf, right?!

We all have our own unique ways to care for our plants and all find a lot of joy in it: "I get really excited when I get new growth and always have to show the boyfriend (whether he wants to see or not)," says Theo. I can see the smile on her face with that one. For Theo, if she sees a plant at a nursery or garden center that she wants, she gets it. You only live once, but I also say that for the plant. So making sure you put the plant's needs first is important.

PLANT SHELF

This kitchen shelf is Theo's favorite plant space—seen here are spotted *Begonia maculata*, satin pothos (*Scindapsus pictus* 'Argyraeus'), *Homalomena rubescens*, and *Rhaphidophora tetrasperma*.

CREATIVE CONTAINERS

I had to get a photo of this cool pot (above)—the *Epiphyllum pittieri* planted in it makes it look like it has hair! On the right, a little terrarium houses a Chinese money plant (*Pilea peperomioides*), with a Madagascar palm (*Pachypodium lamerei*) to the right. The window below is perfect for sun-loving cacti and succulents.

On deciding what room a plant will go in, Theo says, "At this point it's all determined by where there's room." Some would say there's always room for more plants, which sounds like a quote you'd see at a plant shop on a tote bag. However, there isn't always more room because there isn't always more light or more time to care for your plants. What I think is more important is creating a bond with the ones you can care for and focusing on how to make them thrive. Theo sometimes creates bonds with her plants by naming them: "The most recent plant I bought I named Pepper (it's a *Homalomena*)." While she couldn't say which plant is her favorite, she did say, "There are always some I like better than others." Hey, don't judge! This is a judgment-free zone. Theo, I feel you. Believe me.

Lastly, when I asked Theo to share a tip that she's learned on her plant journey, she said, "It's always good to have spare pots in the house. You never know when you're going to need one (cats throwing pots over, plants growing too fast, or you just keep buying more plants, like I do)." She has a point there. Cats are jerks. Sorry. Looks like "great" was autocorrected to "jerks." Well... *c'est la vie.*

PLANT THRONE

Below, Theo has created her very own plant throne. Sitting among the huge *Monstera deliciosa* and *Homalomena rubescens* leaves is the perfect place for a rest. The moody, pale gray walls provide the perfect backdrop for the bright green leaves of the many plants in this room, offset by the 19th-century stucco and original windows. Mid-century furniture is mixed with finds from different eras, but sticking with a natural palette makes everything feel harmonious. Other plants we can see on these pages include Ethiopean asparagus (*Asparagus aethiopicus*) and *Rhipsalis* (opposite, top left), as well as *Begonia rex* and *Anthurium* 'Jungle King' (opposite, top right).

POPS OF COLOR

The couch mimics the softness of the greenery while the rugs add pops of red that complement the flowers on the coffee table and the peach pillow on the couch. Plants on the sideboard opposite include *Philodendron xanadu*, fiddle-leaf fig (*Ficus lyrata*), and *Dracaena*.

A CHARMING BEDROOM
Theo's greenery-filled bedroom makes for a restful night's sleep.
The plants to the right of the bed complement the trees outside
and blur the line between inside and outside. In a closer look at
the plants in the bottom picture on the opposite page, we can
see a burro's tail (*Sedum morganianum*) and a lemon lime *Maranta*.

ART AND PLANTS

Above, this fishbone cactus (*Epiphyllum anguliger*) perfectly picks out the plant motif in the artwork displayed behind it. Repeating shapes, colors, and lines is a great way to layer art, sculptural objects, and plants.

INDOOR/
OUTDOOR

HOME *Sofie Vertongen*
& Yannick De Neef
LOCATION *Antwerp, Belgium*

When you think of Belgium, I'm sure
the one thing you will know is that
they make amazing chocolate. Some
of the best chocolate I've ever had,
honestly. This was no surprise to
me. What did surprise me was how
much I'd love my visit to the city of
Antwerp. That was where I met the
wonderful, plant-loving couple,
Sofie and Yannick. Both born and
raised in Belgium, their love for
plants, interiors, and good food
couldn't measure up to their love
for each other. This much was very
clear. When there is love in a home,
it shows itself in a way that makes
you want to kick off your shoes,
nestle on the couch, and never leave.

"IT'S SO FULFILLING TO TAKE CARE OF YOUR PLANTS, ESPECIALLY
WHEN THEY REWARD YOU WITH A NEW LEAF OR A BEAUTIFUL FLOWER."

So Sofie and Yannick have created this space for themselves and their two cats, Josie and Charlie. In a 2,000 ft² (186 m²) townhouse built in 1905, there's lots of room to create, and better yet, more room for plants. And they do have plenty of them. They purchased their home in the summer of 2018 and started the renovation process, which took a year to complete. They finally got to call it home in the summer of 2019. When I asked them if their plant collection played any role in how they had renovated their home Yannick recalled, "We had two things in mind: creating more space for our cats and plants, and finding new ways to integrate plants into different rooms and lighting conditions." Sofie followed that up with: "We added a beam and skylight in the room downstairs next to the patio so we could add hanging plants and a hanging chair." It's this view into their indoor green room that first takes your breath away. Sofie described their interior style as "a mix of vintage/bohemian/Scandinavian, with lots of green." And by green, it's very obvious what she means. Plants on plants on plants. In my first book, I talked about the importance of creating a plant throne, and here they have taken it to the next level. If I sound envious, it's because I am. Not only did they select the perfect chair for their throne but they also surrounded it with the perfect plants.

Sofie remembers very clearly where her inspiration for greenery first began: "My parents had a big collection of *Yucca* plants in their home, but that was about it. The biggest influence came from my grandfather, who worked in the Botanical Gardens of Meise for his entire working life. His house and garden are filled with all sorts of plants. He still knows the botanical names for all of these plants, and every time we go to visit him, he tells us stories about how much he enjoyed working in the Botanical Gardens." For Yannick, his inspiration came from the bouquets of flowers his father would bring home. He and his father now share the same favorite plant, *Philodendron* 'Moonlight'. It's interesting how much of our love for greenery is handed down. I believe it's because of how nurturing caring for plants is, not to mention how amazing it makes one feel to be surrounded by them. "Plants turn a house into home, and this is exactly what they do for me! Seeing my ficus happy after a hard day's work is just as soothing as the thought of spending the rest of the evening watching a movie on our cozy couch," says Yannick.

One thing I admired about their home was their wonderful eye for detail. Having plants in your home is one thing, but understanding how to style them is another. When I entered their bathroom I was impressed with how well they tied nature in with natural elements—there are wood-framed mirrors, and pebbles make up the wall of the shower. Along with the plants, it's these elements that help blur the line between interior and exterior. "We made the shower wall lower (instead of making it go all the way up to the ceiling), so we could put plants there, too," Sofie says. These ideas can be seen throughout the rest of their home as well. In every room, they have found ways to beautifully tie in plants.

PLANT THRONE
This beautiful hanging chair is the ultimate fantasy of a plant throne. Looking onto the outdoor patio, it's perfectly at home among the plants indoors. Prominent are *Monstera deliciosa* and rubber plant (*Ficus elastica*), as well as a fiddle-leaf fig (*Ficus lyrata*) on the left.

RELAXED LIVING
Opposite, a few well-chosen plants in the dining room include a *Monstera deliciosa* and a bird of paradise (*Strelitzia*). On the left, a little rubber plant (*Ficus elastica*) greets you when you come in the front door, a taste of the plant delights to come!

When I asked Sofie and Yannick how they make decisions on where they'll place plants in their home, Sofie replied, "Some rooms have more light than others, so I make the first selection based on that. And then I just try different options until I feel that it's the 'right' fit for the room. For example, our *Licuala* palm (the palm with round leaves in the bedroom) didn't really fit anywhere until I placed it next to the room divider and then it just made sense and looked great. I can't explain it; it's just a feeling that I get." I can fully understand that feeling. When its right, its right.

While Yannick says his favorite room in the house is their living room because it is home to the plants that have been with them the longest, Sofie and I both love their indoor green room. "It used to be such a

dark area before we tore down the whole wall and put in a big skylight. Now this space is filled with hanging plants and feels like a mini orangery. It's also the perfect spot to enjoy a coffee in the morning, relaxing in the hanging chair with a view of our vertical green wall, just a few feet away outside." This spot in their home is what I would call their "statement piece." But you can't speak about the greatness of the indoor green room without talking about the outdoor patio. This feature of their home is everything. I mean, everything! Not only is it the length of one full wall in the kitchen and one in the green room, two of the walls slide open to create a space that is both outside and inside. When I discussed this space with Sofie she said, "We moved in during the summer and we used it

CATS AND PLANTS
Sophie and Yannick's cat, Charlie, rests on the couch, perfectly at home. Behind her, on a vintage side table, they have a great mix of plants, including: (from left to right) *Polyscias balfouriana*, *Saxifraga stolonifera*, an air plant (*Tillandsia*), dried lavender, and a *Philodendron* 'Florida Ghost' on the shelf below.

almost every day when we were at home. It's so nice to have a drink outside when all the doors are open, and to talk to Yannick while he's cooking in the kitchen. We're planning on maybe adding a small firepit so we can also enjoy the colder winter days outside." Now she's just playing with our emotions.

Sofie and Yannick share their home with two cats that, I must say, they treat and love as if they were children. So for them, making sure the cats can also enjoy the space and plants is important. "Plants tend to have the same effect on our cats as they do on us. They create the relaxed, loving atmosphere that is needed after a hard day's work, and the perfect environment for the tons of cat naps they have over the day!" says Yannick. But, keeping your pets from destroying your plants can sometimes be an issue. Sofie believes they lucked out. "Josie doesn't really care much about the plants, but Charlie likes to bite the grassy ones." While I do think they just ended up with two really sweet cats, I know it's because of their knowledge of plants that their cats don't have any issues. Oh, did I not mention that they own a plant shop? Yes, a plant shop. Not far from where they live, they spend their days in their shop The Plant Corner.

CARE AND FEEDING
Above, Sophie waters a variegated Balfour aralia (*Polyscias scutellaria* 'Balfourii'). Top left, a fishbone cactus (*Epiphyllum anguilger*) and a council tree (*Ficus altissima*) have really different foilage that look great together.

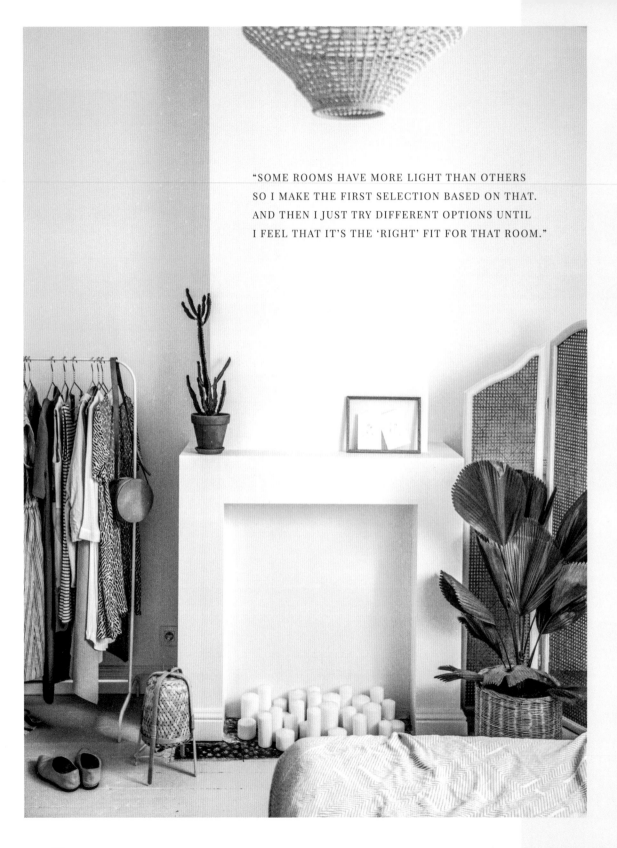

"SOME ROOMS HAVE MORE LIGHT THAN OTHERS
SO I MAKE THE FIRST SELECTION BASED ON THAT.
AND THEN I JUST TRY DIFFERENT OPTIONS UNTIL
I FEEL THAT IT'S THE 'RIGHT' FIT FOR THAT ROOM."

SLEEPING/BATHING

Seen on the right, isn't this a perfectly thought-out idea for how to have more plants in your bathroom? Sofie and Yannick designed the shower wall to stop short of the ceiling so they could use it as a plant ledge—it really shows off the trailing leaves of the *Hoya linearis* and golden pothos (*Epipremnum aureum*). Opposite is a fan palm that didn't look right anywhere until Sofie placed it here; some plants are like that!

"After we moved to Antwerp from Berlin (which is a very green city where everyone has plants), it struck me that it was really a way of life there, because in Antwerp this wasn't the case at all. So, five years ago, I started a webstore where I sold air plants, which turned into us opening our own plant shop after two years of pop-up events and markets. When we opened the shop, it wasn't in a known area or shopping street, so the goal was to make the shop a destination in itself," Sofie recalls. For Yannick, "owning a plant shop also means we get to know 'new' plants almost every week, which makes it a very inspiring job. New plants and possible new colorways obviously have an influence on how you style certain corners of your home." I know what you're thinking, "It's not fair. They own a plant shop so they must never struggle with their plants." But that's not always the case. We all struggle with one plant or another. For Sofie, having ferns indoors tends to give her a problem, but it's her variegated *Monstera deliciosa* that's the real issue: "The white part is always turning brown, even though I don't spray the white leaves and keep it dry between waterings." It's through her dedication and hard work that I'm sure she'll eventually figure it out.

Lastly, I asked them if there was anything they've learned during their journey in greenery that they thought would help us all. Yannick replied, "Owning plants doesn't have to be expensive: just take a cutting from a friend's plant or from your local plant shop, and propagate your plant from scratch." While Sofie said, "Plants really do change the whole vibe of a home. When we had just moved, we brought over all of the furniture first and our plants moved a couple of days after when everything was in place. The house felt really weird and empty without our plants, and it only felt like 'home' once the plants arrived. So my tip would be: if you don't have plants yet, go get some and see for yourself."

THE PLANT CORNER
Sofie and Yannick's plant shop is an oasis in the heart of Antwerp. There are dozens of varieties of plants for sale, as well as unique pots and hanging planters. On the wall are air plants (*Tillandsia*), on top of and in the cabinet are spotted *Begonia maculata*, *Rhaphidophora tetrasperma*, and two *Monstera adansonii*. On the floor on the left and right are baby fiddle-leaf fig (*Ficus lyrata*) plants.

BOHOASIS

HOME *Jesse Maguire*
LOCATION *Chicago, Illinois, USA*

There's so much beauty in Chicago. Particularly if you're visiting in spring or summer—just like the plants we love, the city seems to thrive and bloom during this part of the year. Warm weather and sunlight have that effect on all living things. This happened to be when I got to visit Jesse Maguire, in the 1,295 ft² (120 m²) condo she and her husband Brad share with their pup, Kevin, and their 60 plants. Their condo is on the top floor of a "three flat" (in Chicago, that's what they call a condo in a building with only three units) and sits above many of the other buildings and trees on their block, so they benefit from great light pretty much all day.

"I HAVE NOTICED A SIGNIFICANT CHANGE IN MY OVERALL MOOD SINCE FILLING MY HOME AND TAKING THE TIME TO INTERACT WITH MY PLANTS AS MUCH AS I DO. IT HONESTLY CHANGED MY LIFE."

Jesse describes her style as "always evolving, but a little of Scandi/boho/French-traditional (or at least that's what I'm going for...)" I really relate to the "always evolving" description—I think it's important when styling a home to keep it fresh and try out new things. Just as your plants grow and evolve from season to season, sprinkling a little of that into your decisions when styling your space isn't a bad idea. For Jesse, she pulls inspiration from her work life: "I'm a marketing manager by day for a hospitality group, including restaurants and event spaces, and those gorgeously designed interiors always give me inspiration for what to look for when I thrift," says Jesse. Her reason for starting the process of jungle-fying her home was simple: "I finally had windows! Our old place was so cute but basically a cave. We only had one window that wasn't facing another building. So when we moved in here, I got my first fiddle-leaf fig (killing it slowly over time), but I just kept trying and I can't remember exactly when it all clicked, but I'm sure it was when I saw my first real new growth and then I had the bug. It's a full-blown lifestyle now." Slow down with all the bug talk, Jesse. As plant-lovers, that's the last thing we need... I'm talking to all the mealy bugs out there—but I digress. This is about Jesse and her love for greenery. Growing up in Kentucky, "We definitely had houseplants but I grew up gardening and planting outdoor plants. My mom is an encyclopaedia and always knew all the plant names, and it never really interested me growing up, but I'm sure being around it had an effect subliminally." I love how that particular

moment—when that grow light switches on and a person finally finds their passion for bringing plants indoors—is different for all of us. But when it does switch on, that light floods in, and your life and home are forever changed. For Jesse, "It's one of the things that makes me the happiest in my day-to-day life. I know it sounds dramatic, but I have noticed a significant change in my overall mood since filling my home and taking the time to interact with my plants as much as I do. It honestly changed my life." Jesse, we all feel you!

Once you know and understand the light in your home, and what level of plant care you're comfortable with, bringing in new plants starts to become fun. You're no longer stressing out over your plants dying or not doing as well as they were when you first brought them home. Many people miss this part of the learning process, and just grab any plant they like and start there. For Jesse, knowing what works for her and her home allows her to choose plants more freely: "Sometimes I see one in a store and I just have to have it; sometimes it's because I need a certain look in a certain place, and sometimes its because I've been lusting after a certain variety for a while. It really depends, but I think all are good reasons, which is why I can't stop buying plants. Everything changed when I stopped looking at the plants as a simple decor item and started seeing them as the living things they are. I choose the placement based on the needs of the plant and the light in each room. Once that's all taken into account I can play with how I want to style them."

SHELF LIFE
Jesse created this plant shelf to make use of the light coming in through the window. It's perfect for plants such as the string-of-pearls (*Senecio rowleyanus*) and *Aloe vera*. Opposite, the cool neon-signed bar area in the living room is home to: (from left to right) elephant's ear plant (*Alocasia*), golden pothos (*Epipremnum aureum*), fingertree (*Euphorbia tirucalli*), and a taro (*Colocasia esculenta*).

DIY GENIUS

Below right, a wooden dowel hanging from leather straps is an innovative idea that Jesse came up with for hanging plants. Included in the display are: (from left to right) golden pothos (*Epipremnum aureum*), Christmas cactus (*Schlumbergera*), heart-leaf philodendron (*Philodendron scandens*), *Epipremnum aureum* 'Marble Queen,' and *Philodendron scandens* 'Brasil.' Opposite, a thriving fiddle-leaf fig (*Ficus lyrata*) and a Swiss cheese plant (*Monstera deliciosa*) are loving the light flooding in through the large windows.

Jesse finds a lot of ways to bring DIY projects into her home. She's built beams from wooden dowels and leather straps from which to hang her plants, like living curtains, and I think she's done a great job with the bar corner of the living room. It's just such a nice mix of old and new, color and life. The plant shelf across the window was something Jesse built because of how much light they had coming into the room. It holds various little plants in nice little pots, and adds a great touch to that corner. Jesse loves this area of her home: "That's where most of the plants are and where we spend most of our time. We're lucky to have a full wall of

floor-to-ceiling windows in the room that holds our kitchen, living room, dining area, and bar area, so we can be surrounded by the greenery all the time!" And who wouldn't want that, right?

While Jesse spends a good amount of time caring for her 60 plant babies, there's one lady that watches over it all: her insanely adorable pup, Kevin. Yes, that's right, Kevin is a lady. And through her fur bangs, she peeks out to support her mom in her efforts to care for the plants. When I asked Jesse how Kevin gets along with the plants, she said, "Kevin has never been interested in the plants. She's an older lady, so I'm sure if we ever get another (younger) dog that may change but, currently, we're all getting along."

Once you've become a dedicated plant parent, you start to pick up on certain tips and tricks to make life for you and your green friends much more enjoyable. When I asked her what she's learned over the past few years, Jesse replied: "Remember they are living things that need a lot of attention and interaction to thrive. The most frequently asked question I get on Instagram is 'how do you water them all?' and I think people ask because it looks like a TON of work, and IT IS! I spend hours every week watering, talking to them, repotting, pruning, and I love every minute of it. Lots of people make the mistake of thinking they're bringing a plant in to fit into their lifestyle—and they are, don't get me wrong—but people also need to attend to the plant's needs if you want them to live their best lives!"

KITCHEN CLIMBERS
Jesse has figured out the best way to maximize countertop space in her kitchen: hanging planters. Climbers with diverse foliage, such as *Philodendron scandens* 'Brasil,' string of bananas (*Senecio radicans*), and 'Marble queen' (*Epipremnum aureum*)—range around the kitchen, contributing to the jungle vibe.

MINIMALIST BEDROOM

A few well-chosen and mature plants create calm and focus in the bright bedroom. Above, a horsehead philodendron (*Philodendron bipinnatifidum*) nestles between two windows, while, above right, a heart-leaf philodendron (*Philodendron scandens*) trails its dark green leaves.

JUNGLE LOFT

HOME *Adelyn Duchala*
LOCATION *Philadelphia, Pennsylvania, USA*

In this beautiful loft apartment in Philadelphia, you'll find a space that is defined by its greenery. With only 750 ft² (70 m²) to fill, Adelyn's home would wow any visitor with the way she has creatively found places for every one of the 117 plants she calls her "plant children." This makes perfect sense because she cares for them all with the tenderness and joy that any parent would their child. This is plant parenthood done right. At Adelyn's, I feel completely at ease in a home that is not my own—a rare and exciting feeling.

"I REMEMBER BEING SO FASCINATED WITH PLANTS AT SUCH A YOUNG AGE, AND AS I GOT OLDER, I BEGAN TO DEVELOP A GREAT APPRECIATION FOR THEM AND HOW THEY ADD SUCH A POSITIVE, WONDERFUL ENERGY TO YOUR LIFE AND HOME."

If you were playing "Loft Apartment Bingo" and placed markers on large windows, exposed brick walls, high ceilings, and hardwood floors, well... you'd be onto a winner here: BINGO! For Adelyn, it was these natural elements that attracted her to this apartment, so she could create a space that was uniquely hers.

When asked about how she would describe her style, she replied, "I am not sure if I have a specific style, per se, but my apartment is definitely more of a modern industrial space. I chose to soften the industrial lines by adding a lot of greenery and wood elements with shelving and accent pieces, and I pull in warmer elements wherever I can. I definitely lean more toward a bohemian style, but with a cozy vibe! I need my space to feel bright and open, but warm, comfortable, and peaceful at the same time. I pull a lot of inspiration from nature, and I have always loved Southwestern style, so I definitely let that esthetic inspire my personal space." Amen to that! Her inspiration and passion for the idea of "home" is ever-present in how she styles and curates her space.

As easy as it may seem, being able to create a space that doesn't feel cluttered or accidental is an art. You need a real keen eye not only to understand what plants will look great in your space, but also which will work well when layered with each other. As a photographer, Adelyn has spent many years developing her eye: "I have always had a love of photographing nature, and a hidden passion for home styling, and developing and curating an esthetic within

my own space. I currently work as the creative photographer for Terrain, but initially started my career there as a stylist, which I would say definitely allowed me to fine-tune my style, and how I look at the elements within my own home. Life-styling and photographing home products and plants for a living has inspired me to try new things when it comes to styling, and just to constantly see my space as if I were going to be photographing it with my camera."

Having spent the past five years bringing the outside in, the last two and a half years have been when she truly went wild. There's always a trigger or some sort of spark that turns someone from having just a few plants into becoming the proud keeper of a fully fledged indoor jungle. I know for me, it was my move to New Orleans that sparked this inspiration. For Adelyn, it was a slow burn that started as a kid: "I have been able to bring in a lot more plants due to the amount of space and light that my current home provides. I have always had an immense love and deep connection to nature. My mom always had houseplants or a flower garden outside that she would be tending to. I would definitely say that my grandmother was my biggest plant influencer growing up. She always had so many houseplants, and beautiful flower gardens and containers outside... Growing up, my family and I moved around about every four years or so, and I was never able to establish this connection or this "feeling" of home in each place we were living at the time. However, since I was about seven, my

GREEN LIVING AND WORKING

On the previous page, Adelyn's office is anything but a boring workspace, as the trailing silver philodendron (*Scindapsus pictus* 'Exotica') that she propagated has claimed the brick wall. Not only is this beauty easy to care for, it also grows super fast. With high ceilings throughout her apartment, Adelyn can grow large plants such as the bird of paradise (*Strelitzia*) seen on the left. A weeping jade (*Senecio jacobsenii*), an air plant (*Tillandsia*), and a *Hoya carnosa* are all thriving on the shelf above.

brother and I would spend our entire summer in Upstate New York on Cayuga Lake at my grandparents' house, where we would be outside in the woods, or on the lake, or out hiking in the gorges, and this became the only constant in my life. Especially being in the city where you aren't surrounded by as much nature—that was something I missed tremendously. So, I created a small greenhouse in my home instead!"

Creating your own personal greenhouse can be super rewarding, that's for sure. But understanding what types of plants will thrive in your space and how to care for them can be demanding. So, when it comes to purchasing new plants, you have to have a plan. Adelyn says, "When I'm shopping for new plants, I definitely gravitate toward whatever plant is 'calling' me. I know that sounds silly, but sometimes you just feel drawn to certain plants for no reason at all, and then can't imagine your life without them! But, when I see a plant I love, I always run through a list of questions before I make the commitment: how large will this plant grow to be (if you are purchasing it when it is small), do I have space for this plant in my home as it is now, or when it grows? I also consider the type of light it needs and determine exactly where I can put it in my home. If you are unable to provide the correct light and care for a plant, there is no reason to bring it home—it will all end in sadness. My living room gets perfect light. This is direct bright morning light, and for the rest of the day, indirect light. My ceilings

are very tall, so I don't have to worry too much about plant height. But, my bedroom and bathroom are fairly dark. My bedroom has a snake plant (*Sansevieria trifasciata*), two ZZ plants (*Zamioculcas zamiifolia*), and a low-light, pothos variety that all do very well from the light which creeps in through the doorway and through the skylight on the ceiling. If I am able to say 'yes' to all these questions, if I know I have the space and can provide the correct care for the plant, I then think about how it will fit in esthetically. When I was shopping for the two empty corners in my living room, I knew I wanted a large-scale plant to really fill up the space height-wise, but one that was also easy to care for and could add drama to the corner—and the bird of paradise (*Strelitzia*) was the perfect plant for that! I always think about the scale of the plant and what it will look like when it grows while I am shopping for specific areas of my home. But sometimes you just have to bring home whatever plant is speaking to you in that moment!" With Adelyn's 117 plants, that's a lot of talking going on at once. Yes, plants do talk: they speak to each other in the way they move and grow and through the color of their foliage. If they are bright and vibrant in color, they are happy and doing well, but if their color starts to fade or changes to yellow or brown, something is definitely wrong. Understanding this is important as a plant parent, but picking a favorite child is never an easy ask.

Adelyn continues: "I love them all. But if I had to pick a favorite, or two, or four... I would go

with *Monstera deliciosa*, because it grows fairly quickly with the right light, and it's just so stunning! It's truly a plant that has that 'wow' factor when you walk into a room. I also love jade plants and weeping jades. They are so unique and easy to care for, once you remember not to overwater them. I also have a soft spot in my heart for ferns. I don't have too many because they can be quite difficult to care for—they are a little needy—but there is just something so delicate and soft about them. My Grandma always had ferns, so that is probably why they feel so special to me. And satin pothos (*Scindapsus pictus* 'Argyraeus') as well as silver

philodendron (*Scindapsus pictus* 'Exotica') are just so effortlessly cool, and super easy to care for and propagate. I am a sucker for any trailing plant, and those guys just take off!
I have a whole bunch of them, mostly all from the same two plants that I propagated, and my one silver guy just decided to start growing up my brick wall one day, and claimed its space rather quickly!"

It's one thing to care for all of your indoor plants but getting the chance to grow them outdoors as well is what really made me envious of Adelyn's space: "I am lucky enough to have an outdoor space which I truly cherish in the spring,

JUNGLE LIVING ROOM

The living room gets eastern light, which is direct morning light, and indirect light for the rest of the day—the perfect environment for many plants. Opposite, a *Monstera adansonii* and satin pothos (*Scindapsus pictus* 'Argyraeus') trail from shelves; and above, a large Swiss cheese plant (*Monstera deliciosa*) casts its delicate shade over the couch.

"NATURE, AND BEING OUTDOORS, IMPACTED ME IN SUCH A LARGE WAY GROWING UP, AND IT HAS ALWAYS GIVEN ME A SENSE OF BEING HOME, THIS NEED TO BRING NATURE INTO MY HOME WAS ALWAYS SOMETHING I NEEDED TO FUEL THIS DEEP CONNECTION WITHIN."

LIVING KITCHEN

Adelyn's apartment shows
how open-plan living optimizes
available space. A white kitchen
island separates the living room
from the kitchen, which receives
the same perfect plant-growing
light as the living room. Hanging
plants are great for a kitchen—
they thrive in the water vapor
and warmth, and make great
use of space, which can be at
a premium in a city kitchen.
Adelyn's *Monstera adansonii*
and satin pothos (*Scindapsus
pictus* 'Argyraeus') look right
at home here, trailing their
beautiful leaves over white
cabinets that provide a simple
backdrop for the greenery.

GALLERY WALL
Adelyn's artistic eye can be seen at work in how she has mounted striking specimens of staghorn fern (*Platycerium*) on her gallery wall. In doing so, she has transformed these gnarly plants into abstract pieces of art that are perpetually a work in progress. A large rubber plant (*Ficus elastica*) in a woven grass pot and a spiky *Aloe vera* frame the scene.

summer, and fall. I move a lot of my plants outdoors as it gets warmer, and also have some planted flowers. This space provides a really great little escape. Being able to be outdoors in the fresh air, surrounded by all of my plants and flowers, I sometimes forget I am in the city, and it feels like this little jungle oasis that can extend from my indoors, outdoors!"

Bringing plants in and out could be pretty difficult when it comes to care, one would think. For Adelyn, "It's actually not as stressful as you would think, unless you forget to check you aren't bringing any other little critters into your home! One summer, I forgot to spray my plants/check the soil and had a small colony of spiders make their way into my home for fall. I always make sure to check my plants for bugs, and to make sure I have the right amount of space for those plants that really grew throughout the summer months. Moving plants such as succulents, cacti, or tropical plants back inside also requires a different watering

pattern—they won't need as much water as they did when they were exposed to the outdoor sunlight, so being mindful of that is really important. I also try to pay attention to how much light my plants were getting while living on my deck, and let this determine where I place them when they are brought back indoors. For example, if they were in full sun outside, I will keep them in a sunnier spot within my apartment so that they aren't completely 'shocked' when they come back inside for the winter." These are all things you might learn as you grow with your green friends. Trial and error will always be a part of the process, but make sure to lput those lessons learned to good use.

When I asked Adelyn to choose one thing she's learned over the past few years, she said, "Definitely to be realistic about what you are able to care for and to be sensitive to the specific care that each plant requires. I always do my research on each plant before I bring it into my home. This changed everything for

LUSH FOLIAGE
Beautiful, healthy plants, all living their best lives. Succulents and cacti seen in the top photo thrive in the bright sun, as do taro (*Colocasia esculenta*) and horsehead philodendron (*Philodendron bipinnatifidum*) in the photo above.

me! Knowing how often to water your plants as well as what kind of soil and light is preferred—overwatering was definitely my downfall in the beginning of my plant journey, and so many of my plants struggled because I wasn't paying attention to what each one needed. Once you tune in to the needs of each plant, it will become an intuitive connection, where you will just know if they need something!" I love hearing this type of passion and understanding from someone in the plant community. Having that connection with your plants is everything. For me it was life-changing. For Adelyn: "Truly, I can't imagine not having plants in my home—they just bring me so much joy and happiness. I strive to create a space that not only inspires me each and every day, but also a space that brings me peace and evokes a calmness from within—and my plants do just that. I immediately feel so much more at ease when I step into my home—I love just being able to take a deep breath and relax. While some may step into my home and think I have my work cut out for me—which I do at times—there is something special about caring for plants; it is definitely a form of meditation for me and re-centers me every day." I feel you, Adelyn. I. Feel. You!

THE DECK
Adelyn's deck is a sunny spot for plants to hang out in the summer, before moving back inside for the winter. Peeking through the bird of paradise (*Strelitzia*) leaves, we can see a prickly pear (*Opuntia*), on the left, and a bowl of succulents on the coffee table.

BEYOND
LOW LIGHT

HOME *Marissa McInturff
& Curro Bernabeu*
LOCATION *Barcelona,
Catalonia, Spain*

As someone who loves bringing greenery indoors and styling plants in a way that makes a space feel electric and lush, I take pride in finding amazing planters for my plants to pose in. I think of planters like a plant's outfit—they allow a plant to express its shape, color, texture, and uniqueness. Planters such as those made by Architectural Pottery in the 1950s have inspired me for some time. So, when my friend Nooni Reatig, an architect herself, told me about her friend Marissa McInturff, a ceramic artist living in the beautiful city of Barcelona, and I saw the amazing planters she made, I knew I needed one in my life. But it wasn't until Nooni suggested I go see Marissa's home—which she shares with her husband Curro, their three cats Pepe, Pingui, and Ines, and their many, many plant friends, that the circle would finally be complete.

Curro and Marissa purchased their home about two years ago, "Our building was constructed in the late 1930s, and we're not sure of its original purpose—it could have been housing, a workshop, or a warehouse. Everyone we talk to has a different theory," says Marissa. Their home has about 750 ft² (70 m²) of indoor space, but the real magic is in the 800 ft² (74 m²) of outdoor space. When you first enter their building, you are in a linear atrium that connects four units. The atrium is covered with frosted glass which helps to filter bright indirect light into the space throughout the day. Because of this, the residents of the building place plants outside their doors to make the communal spaces a lush, welcoming environment. Once you enter the apartment, you can feel the effect of the Mediterranean location right away. Warm and vibrant colors pop from every angle, while texture and shape frame it all. From the archways that lead from one room to another, to the collection of Scandinavian light fixtures, to the basket woven animal heads that grace the exposed brick walls, and the beauty of Marissa's ceramic planters, the vibes here are very much what you'd expect from the home of two artists. Marissa describes their home as an "art-filled urban *masia* (a *masia* is a typical farmhouse here in Catalonia). We're both artists and have very distinct (and very different) styles, so it's been a fun challenge to mix the two. I'm a ceramicist and Curro is a filmmaker, and there's evidence of both of those worlds everywhere in our home."

What I didn't expect was the surprisingly low level of light that actually enters their home. The few windows they do have look onto the patio and atrium, so, for them, bringing the outside in had more to do with filling their home with natural elements like wooden flooring, woven rugs, furniture, and art, and the occassional plant. Working with low to medium light, they have sprinkled plants like ponytail palm (*Beaucarnea recurvata*), snake plant (*Sansevieria trifasciata*), and ZZ plant (*Zamioculcas zamiifolia*) throughout. "That's been a real learning process for us, especially since our last apartment was much brighter. We've done a lot of research and often ask our plant expert friends what would be happiest in our not-especially-bright space. There's also been some trial and error—we'll bring something in and observe it, and if it's not happy, we'll move it to a brighter area. The climate here is pretty mild, and we have a lot of bright, protected outdoor spaces for plants to go if they don't like the conditions inside the house," says Marissa. So because of this, they let their outdoor spaces showcase their passion for greenery. And are they ever—passionate! When I asked Marissa how many plants they care for she just said, "Hundreds." I didn't dare count for myself—seeing plants protruding from every corner, windowsill, and wall of their patios and terrace, I just took her word for it. They have been bringing plants home since the day they moved in: "Immediately after moving in (and we do this a couple of times a year), we rented

CLIMBING UP THE WALL
On the patio wall on the right are spider plants (*Chlorophytum comosum*), a Boston fern (*Nephrolepis exaltata*), and *Philodendron scandens* 'Brasil.' Above left, Curro misting a Madagascar jasmine (*Stephanotis floribunda*). Above, a cat hiding behind a ponytail palm (*Beaucarnea recurvata*).

a van and drove up the coast to one of our favorite nurseries (in Spanish, it's called a *vivero*) and absolutely filled the van, top to bottom, wall-to-wall with plants. Our last apartment had a tiny balcony, and now we have a ton of outdoor space, but it's all paved, so our immediate need was to fill it up with green! There wasn't even a question, it was just this need. Both of us love the outdoors and crave a connection with nature, and having plants in our home gives us that." Curro told me he grew up in a home with houseplants, but definitely not quite as many as they have now. For Marissa, there were fewer inside, but she grew up in a home with lots of windows that was surrounded by trees. She said, "Although the green wasn't inside, the connection to it was very strong."

Living in Barcelona has its benefits. You get to eat all of the *paella*, take siestas, and have mild to warm weather all year round. This means you rarely have to bring your outdoor plants inside once winter shows its ugly face. For Marissa and Curro, this is everything because they treat their patios and terrace like an extension of their living/dining rooms. Since they mostly purchase plants for their outdoor spaces, there are many more options to choose from. For them, shopping for plants is quite simple: "It's often based on love at first sight. Once we get a plant home, then we figure out where to put it. But at other times, we'll be looking for something for a specific space and need to be sure we find a plant that will be happy with the light conditions," says Marissa. With so many

ARTISTS' HOME
Beautiful paintings, prints, and sculptures adorn Marissa and Curro's home. As the indoors has quite low light, plants such as the dragon tree (*Dracaena draco*) do well here.

plants, they have never felt the need to name them, and when asked, they wouldn't admit to having a favorite, although Marissa says, "To be honest, Curro has a soft spot in his heart for the ponytail palms (especially the one he rescued from the trash)." As they say, "One man's trash ponytail palm is another man's treasured ponytail palm"—or something like that.

Moving through their home felt so relaxing. While I loved everything about their dining room, I have to agree with Marissa's answer when I asked her what her favorite green space was: "Probably our lower patio because, although it's outside, you can see it from almost every room. Also, it makes the whole house feel so much greener." She's right—the lower patio is where the gradation of that indoor/outdoor line first happens. There is just so much to take in out there. And if you look closely, you might find one of their cats peering out at you, as Curro and Marissa have created a special oasis for themselves and their three cats.

When I asked what they'd learned from taking care of their plants, Marissa said, "You don't need to have a space that's absolutely bathed in light to be able to have plants. Discovering snake plants and trailing philodendrons has been a revelation for us... they're so happy in the low, indirect light they get here, and both are so sculptural. We're bringing more in all the time." I love discoveries of what works best for you, your space, and the plants you bring into your home. Thank you for those wise words, my friends.

OUTDOOR ROOMS

The patios and terrace benefit from bright light and mild temperatures all year round, and are the perfect home for hundreds of varieties of plants. A few of my favorites are shown in the photograph above: olive trees (*Olea europaea*), and *Euphorbia trigona*. Above right, Marissa's handmade pots are home to some tiny succulents.

LET THE LIFE/ LIGHT IN

HOME *Latisha Carlson*
LOCATION *Albuquerque, New Mexico, USA*

As a kid, I thought the only thing living in the New Mexico desert was the roadrunner from the Looney Tunes cartoons—I figured not much more than that. I was young and naïve and, honestly, back then I couldn't point out New Mexico on a map if I tried. Let me tell you, after visiting, there's a lot of living happening in New Mexico—to be more specific, in the town of Albuquerque and in the home Latisha (Tish) shares with her husband Matt, their twin girls, Audrey and Kelsey, son Greyson, and my favorite Goldendoodle west of the Mississippi river, Lemon. They live in a 2,000 ft² (186 m²) brick home that was built in the 1950s, and have been renovating it for the last nine years. Since moving in, they've been working on getting the vibes right—refreshing the decor and feel of the space is something Tish really enjoys.

Tish would describe her style as "a mix between bohemian/mid-century/ Southwestern." It's the Southwestern style that seems to burn brighter here than everywhere else. Tish has the mood down pat, but being able to tie all of these styles together takes a creative eye. For her, its right there. She can see it: "I'm involved in so many avenues of creativity. I am a photographer, influencer, shop owner, creative director, product stylist, and interior designer. I become inspired in many ways and through that I apply it all in different ways throughout my home and, cross my fingers, it makes sense." Believe me, it does. Room to room, each ties together like a bow. Or better yet, a bolo tie.

With a full house of people—and let's not forget Lemon—Tish provides care for about 150 plants. Unlike me, she doesn't name her plants— I mean, 150 is a lot to remember. She just refers to them as her "plant babies." While it might be a desert outside, it's a jungle inside. Tish finds all the right moments to get wild at home. I mean come on, I had to drop that line in at least once in this book—sorry, not sorry. But enough about me and back to Tish. When I asked her how long she has been living with plants, she said, "Funny story: several years ago I began with a few plants and ended up killing them. So I tried again, and I killed those as well. Matt told me I shouldn't buy any more, which we laughed about. Fast-forward a couple years and I found myself in our tiny home in Arizona (we spent a year there), and I began filling that

space up with plants. Everything stayed alive there, and so when we moved back to our New Mexico home, I brought back all our plants from Arizona and began adding more and more. For someone who battles severe anxiety and depression, I learned that bringing the outdoors in brought life to me. I began replacing small knickknack items with plants. Less is more, and to me adding plants looked less busy than all the 'things.'" The power of greenery, right?! I love that. At a young age, Tish remembers her mother spending hours working on their garden outside, but found it funny that all of their indoor plants were fake, "In the last couple of years I have inspired her to replace all her fake plants with living ones, and she is in love," says Tish. My mother also had fake plants in the house when I was a kid, and my grandmother covered all of the living room furniture in plastic —but that's a story for another time.

To tell the story of Tish's home, you'd have to start with how beautifully styled each room is. There's a consistency in color and tone, and style, too. While each room seems to have its own theme, all have the same Southwestern style at their core. There's beauty in her living room with its vaulted ceiling, leather couch, and lush surroundings. There's a touch of whimsy and charm in each of the children's rooms. But my favorite room in the house has to be her living room, which is the first room you walk into once you enter. Here, the wallpaper print is the most colorful part of the home, while the furnishings grab your attention with their size

MAKE AN ENTRANCE

Tish's entryway is a perfectly composed still life—I love all the natural textures, from the shaggy pillow to the cermaic vases. The majestic snake plant (*Sansevieria trifasciata*) sets it all off. Opposite, the jungle wallpaper blurs the line between indoors and outdoors, tying in well with the marble column (*Euphorbia trigona*)on its right.

and boldness. The entire setup is well thought-out and begs guests to find a moment to relax. This room doesn't get the most light, so Tish anchors the space with a large horsehead philodendron (*Philodendron bipinnatifidum*), and adds another bit of life with a *Monstera*-print pillow on the couch. I enjoy chatting with fellow plant-lovers/stylists about their choices for where to place a plant and what type of plant to place. For Tish, "I think about the light, width, and height of the rooms. I think about what texture and color the plants are, and how to add that in different ways." This is the right way to go about it. Consider the life of the plant first and, in doing so, you'll find its place in your home.

As I spent time with Tish and her family, sharing stories about life and plant care, I wanted her to share

something she's learned over the past years of being a plant parent. In her opinion: "I hear too often that people say 'I kill plants so I can't have them' or 'I really want plants but I am too nervous.' I would just say to add plants! Don't let the plant you killed stop you, and don't let your worry about keeping one alive stop you from adding plants to your home. Find your favorite plant shop and ask questions, do some research to learn, start with an easy plant, and add more as you learn. Remember, I killed many plants before my house became a jungle—and I even own a plant shop now. Also, know that I have lost some plants since then. It happens, but plants make a space happier, so find what suits you and your home." I love so much of what Tish says, but I would also add a small caveat: yes, we've all killed a plant, but don't make a habit of it

IT'S A JUNGLE
The plants in this room create a lush vibe. From left to right, we have *Monstera deliciosa*, *Alocasia*, staghorn fern (*Platycerium*), *Philodendron* 'Pink Princess,' fiddle-leaf fig (*Ficus lyrata*), *Euphorbia eritrea* 'Variegata', *Yucca*, and a rubber plant (*Ficus elastica*).

SOUTHWESTERN CRAFTS
Tish uses handmade textures to contrast with the bright green foliage of her plants. On the left, *Monstera deliciosa* specimens are kings of the dining room. Below, an umbrella tree (*Schefflera actinophylla*) hangs out over the sink, on the right we get a glimpse of a horsehead philodendron, as well as Lemon, the Goldendoodle.

just to have a home filled with greenery. Remember, PLANTS ARE LIVING THINGS and should be treated as such. I would suggest that the best thing to do if you're feeling a bit nervous or unsure is to do what Tish says when it comes to research. Start there—find out what type of light your home or room gets, and research what types of plants thrive in that sort of light. Remember, that plant didn't ask to be brought home with you. It was living a perfectly wonderful life at the nursery or plant shop you found it in. You took the decision to make it a part of your life, now it's your time to do the work of caring for it and treating it like another member of your family.

"I LEARNED THAT BRINGING THE OUTDOORS IN BROUGHT LIFE TO ME."

THE REAL BED, BATH, AND BEYOND

Plant shelves above a bed are a great way to bring greenery to a bedroom. Trailing plants such as golden pothos (*Epipremnum aureum*), *Epipremnum aureum* 'Neon,' staghorn fern (*Platycerium*), and air plants (*Tillandsia* species) are perfect here. Below right, a Boston fern (*Nephrolepis exaltata*) and a snake plant (*Sansevieria trifasciata*) are loving the humidity of the bathroom. Below left, a rubber plant (*Ficus elastica*) is thriving in the bright light next to a window.

PLAYFUL SPACES

In Tish's children's rooms, the plants blend
seamlessly with fun artworks and soft textures.
Opposite is a horsehead philodendron
(*Philodendron bipinnatifidum*) in a standing
pot. Above, a rubber plant (*Ficus elastica*) sits
next to a small *Monstera deliciosa*, while above
right, a heart-leaf philodendron (*Philodendron
scandens*) hangs above a bed. Finally, on the
right, we have a dragon tree (*Dracaena*) and
a ZZ plant (*Zamioculcas zamiifolia*).

THE MINIMALIST

HOME *Joel Bernstein*
LOCATION *Kilburn, London, UK*

I know, you're probably wondering where Joel's portrait is. But he's there. If you look closely, he's right there. He is the image. He's every bit of it. The emerald-green tiles against the concrete walls, the small green stove with the pink and green *Syngonium* on top, picking out the colors in the fabric on the chair across from it. There he is. The details here and across the following pages will give you a clear picture of exactly what defines interior curator Joel Bernstein. That's the magic of his home. In this beautiful cottage in Kilburn, London, Joel has curated a space uniquely his own.

"JOEL'S HOME IS NOT A MUSEUM AND HE DOESN'T WANT
IT TREATED AS SUCH—HE WANTS EVERY PART OF IT TO
BE EXPLORED, TOUCHED, AND EXPERIENCED."

Growing up in Cape Town, South Africa, had a huge impact on Joel's esthetic—living next to the sea and seeing a lot of blue sky really inspired him, and his home in northwest London is a testament to that. You see, unlike most British folk, Joel's approach to decorating is very cozy and bright. When I asked him to describe his style, he said it was "textured, muted, colorful, and artisanal." which can clearly be seen in these images. But what he wanted to make sure I noted was that he "always prioritizes comfort above everything else."

As you move throughout his home, what truly vibrates is how passionate he is about making every bit of the space a work of art in its own right. His love for collecting handmade objects and natural finds is displayed on the many tables around his home.

As they say, there's a place for everything and everything has its place. That is very true for how Joel brings greenery into his home. Although he is a maximalist when it comes to the objects and art he displays, it is very clear that he is a minimalist when it comes to plants. While his outdoor garden is lush with hundreds of varieties of plants, he has just 20 indoors, bringing in bits of greenery where it feels right and doing what makes sense for the plants. The importance of that self-awareness is everything—Joel understands that it isn't quantity over quality.

Having plants in his life has always felt natural to Joel, and while he didn't grow up with plants indoors, he was surrounded by beautiful

gardens. He told me that he used to have many more plants in his home but has transitioned the majority to live outdoors. The plants that have remained inside all need an indoor environment to survive.

Shopping mostly in specialist nurseries, Joel has a wish list of indoor plants, many of which are quite rare plants. Joel does not appreciate them specifically for their rarity, however it's more about what they represent to him, and how they grow. He especially likes "the element of surprise" with plants that are not like any other plants—he doesn't like to have plants that are overexposed. This I took to mean "trendy" plants. In particular, Joel is always on the lookout for tubular *Euphorbia* but says they are difficult to come across in the UK.

There are so many inspiring rooms in Joel's home—I found myself walking around with a goofy smile on my face because I was just so taken by everything I saw. I thought about what I wanted for myself in life and felt happy for someone who had obtained it. Joel's living room, with its high ceilings, whitewashed wooden floors, and beautiful skylights is everything I'd ever want—it's in his living room that I found my true bit of calm, and where you'll find the most greenery.

For Joel, his favorite room is the modern kitchen extension that he added to the existing home, which had been a Victorian artist's studio. He wanted the kitchen to be in keeping with the original building, but also have the feeling of a cottage in a woodland.

"I LIKE THE ELEMENT OF SURPRISE
THAT COMES WITH RARE PLANTS.
I DON'T LIKE TO HAVE PLANTS THAT
ARE OVEREXPOSED."

A LIGHT-FILLED LIVING ROOM

Believe it or not, it was actually raining outside
when these photographs were taken! Joel's
home is a plant-lover's dream because of how
much light the large windows and skylights let in.
Most people would fill these rooms with as many
plants as they could squeeze in. But not Joel—just
like all the other pieces in his home, his plants are
very carefully curated. A large bird's-nest fern
(*Asplenium nidus*), a ponytail palm (*Beaucarnea
recurvata*), and an asparagus fern (*Asparagus
setaceus*), a South African plant—all in stately
pots—create a sophisticated atmosphere.

THE GARDEN BEYOND

Opposite, the doors leading
to the garden create a picture
window of the lush greenery
beyond. Positioned between two
comfortable chairs, an African
hemp (*Sparrmannia africana*)
unfurls its soft leaves. It is this
simplicity, color palette, and
placement that create an image
of who Joel Bernstein is. It's not
just about one item, but about
the whole picture.

It's in the kitchen that Joel spends most of his time in the summer, with friends constantly coming in and out. To blur that line between interior and exterior, he loves sitting at the table and having the doors in the kitchen open to the garden all summer long. He says that he used to keep the doors open all night, too, until an urban fox came in one night. He put an end to that soon after—I think we all would!

KITCHEN SCENES

Benefitting from huge skylights and doors to the garden, Joel's kitchen is a soothing space. Tiny specimens of *Mimosa pudica* and jade plant (*Crassula ovata*) sit on the table, while opposite, a rare and beautiful Hawaiian palm (*Brighamia insignis*) sits on the countertop.

SMALL WONDER

HOME *Whitney Leigh Morris & Adam Winkleman*
LOCATION *Venice, California, USA*

There aren't many families out there doing small-space living better than the family at The Tiny Canal Cottage. This lovely, one-bedroom, American Craftsman-style cottage, located close to the canals in Venice, is the home of Whitney and Adam, their three-year-old son, West, and their two pups StanLee and Sophie. Yes, you counted right. That's two grown adults, a young kid, and two medium-sized dogs in a home a little bit less than 400 ft² (37 m²). I was curious about how they made it work, but, after getting to know them, I totally understood. It's pretty simple. Their home, as small as it is, is full of love. When you love the people you're with as much as they love each other, sharing a space as small as theirs comes easily.

> "FOR ME, PERSONALLY, OUR PLANTS HAVE A GROUNDING EFFECT, AND MAKE ME FEEL LIKE THE HOUSE IS WHOLE."

One reason it's easier for the family to live in a small house is because it's also Whitney's job: "I'm a small-space living consultant and blogger, and I run my business from our tiny home. As such, our personal space and my professional work overlap 24 hours a day… for better and worse." When I visited, I was amazed by the choreographed dance I saw taking place throughout their home. One person steps here so another can step there… one two, step, one two, step. There's no secret as to why Whitney describes her style as "simple, but not minimal. Inspired by nature and multi-purpose functionality." So, when living in such a small space, every item must have a real purpose or it just wouldn't work.

For them, surrounding themselves with greenery had to extend beyond the walls of the home and into their outdoor space. When it comes to having plants, she says "Indoors, we typically have around 12. Our outdoor space is small, but we have about 90 plants spread throughout our garden, stoops, and porch. We want our home to feel like it has a pulse of its own, and what better way to do that than with plants. However, it doesn't take much for a small home or apartment to feel cluttered—especially in a live/work/play space such as ours. For the most part, we go vertical when arranging our plants, suspending them from walls, higher surfaces, and sometimes even the ceiling beams. We also have an oversized variegated rubber plant that sits on our kitchen counter. It's not only a beautiful statement piece, but it also serves as a privacy barrier between our ever-open kitchen window and our neighbor's home. Without plants, the house feels stagnant and sparse. When it rains I relocate the indoor plants all at once for a collective outdoor bath, and while they're absent the interior is sapped of its warmth and originality," explains Whitney.

When I asked her if she grew up with plants, she ecstatically replied, "Yes, yes, yes—and I'm still appreciative of it, decades later. I grew up in north Florida, under oak trees dripping with Spanish moss (hence the moss sculpture in our main room), surrounded by endless stretches of green and bodies of water. My parents made sure that the life around us didn't stop at the exterior walls of our home—they ushered it indoors with an atrium that overflowed with trees and potted plants, along with scattered greenery they tended to with great affection." Having this type of upbringing must bring so much wonder to a young person, but it's as an adult that you start to understand the benefits. For me, I didn't realize the joys of bringing greenery indoors until the age of 34. For Whitney, "I began to appreciate the impact of indoor greenery a decade ago and have been weaving it into my space ever since. As our family has become more environmentally conscientious, we've found ourselves outfitting our home with far fewer belongings, and more plants. We've also begun composting, adding dried leaves and clippings to our tumbler every week to create nutrient-rich soil for the outdoor plants. I suppose it's our little way of cutting back on waste and regenerating life as best we can in this compact setting." If you feel as I do, you probably now want Whitney and her family to be your best friends, too.

VARIEGATED VARIETIES
Whether it's the rubber plant,
Ficus elastica 'Doescheri,' next to
their refrigerator, the ivy and creeping
figs hanging around the living room,
or the arrowhead vine (*Syngonium
podophyllum*)—Whitney's favorite—on
top of the desk, their plants often have
a splash of white and a dash of green.

While Whitney has found ways to make small-space living work for them and help guide other families to better living, I couldn't help but wonder what the relationship was like between their son West and the plants they have inside and out. As someone who doesn't have kids yet, I tend to wonder what that addition would do to the plant family I have now. I've heard horror stories of friends' kids ripping entire branches off plants in fits of rage or pouring extra water into planters while parents weren't watching, thinking they're helping, only to overwater a plant. With West, Whitney says that it's kind of a delicate balance. "West really enjoys gardening and watching leaves, fruit, veggies, herbs, and flowers grow. He regularly asks to water the indoor and outdoor plants,

and he's great at it (he even has a gardening apron that he puts on before tackling the task). But numerous dangling vines above our bed are sometimes too much for him to resist. Occasionally, he'll jump up and gleefully pull a pot down. (For him, it's not an attempt to hurt the plants—I think he's just thrilled that he's tall enough to jump so high and reach them on his own.) I'm confident he'll get past that urge soon. I hope he continues to find joy in putting on his apron and taking care of the plants for years to come."

What I've realized after meeting a lot of people in the plant community, is how particular some can be about the plants they collect. Moving through Adam and Whitney's home, you'll notice that most of the indoor plants they've brought in seem to be of the

variegated variety. When I asked Whitney about this she said, "Our main room is filled with texture but has a subdued color palette, so I prefer variegated plants in there to bolster the texture and enrich the tones. Our bedroom is a bit busier visually, so I usually lean toward leaves with more uniform tones to soothe the eye. Shape is a primary consideration for me when plant shopping—mainly due to the small size of our cottage. My aim is for the plants to become part of the house, just as much as the built-ins and windows."

Plants becoming a part of their home doesn't only mean the interior; they also utilize their outside space just as much. Understanding which plants will work outdoors is vital, but knowing when outside plants need to come indoors and vice versa is a must. "We work with the seasons and sunlight patterns when deciding what plants to put in the garden, and whether to plant or pot them. Southern California is almost perpetually in some state of drought, so we strive to be conservative with our water use and select plants accordingly," says Whitney.

When I asked her to leave us with one last tip she's learned she said, "I've learned homes don't have to be brimming with the latest decor trends to be stylish—on the contrary, actually. We can lower our environmental footprint by buying fewer mass-produced home goods that we don't need, instead investing in living greenery that will clean our air, indoors and out, while beautifying our spaces in a uniquely magical way." Now those are words to live by.

MUTED TONES
Opposite, some clever storage above the bed accommodates a heart-leaf philodendron (*Philodendron scandens*)—not variegated because of the busier design of the bedroom. Above right, a dreamy view into the garden.

INDOOR/OUTDOOR
The garden and all the other outside areas of Whitney's home are where over 90 of her plants hang out. Taking advantage of the sunny and warm climate of southern California, this is a real haven and a space to get away from the bustle of Venice.

DROUGHT-FRIENDLY GARDENING

Whitney is very sensitive to the climate and constant droughts that are a regular part of life in California, and so chooses plants that require minimal watering. Succulents, cacti, and horsehead philodendron (*Philodendron bipinnatifidum*), below, all thrive here.

CLEAN & GREEN

HOME *Dee Campling*
LOCATION *Cheltenham,
Gloucestershire, UK*

Just a two-hour train ride west of
London, in the town of Cheltenham,
is where I found interior designer,
Dee Campling. Cheltenham is on
the edge of the Cotswolds, a
naturally beautiful part of England.
Coming into town, I gazed out of
my train window at rolling green
hills and wide-open blue sky.
The day was just right for a visit to
Dee's lovely home. When I entered,
I came in via the kitchen, which
is at the back of the house and the
brightest and most open room in
the home. The first thing I took
notice of was how many plants
there are in the kitchen. Because
this part of the house has so many
windows, skylights, and just
wonderful overall light, this area
has the most greenery and also
helps blur that line we always talk
about: the one between inside
and outside.

> "I LOVE HOW PLANTS CAN INSTANTLY CHANGE THE
> LOOK OF A ROOM AND ADD COLOR AND TEXTURE."

Dee lives in a classic Victorian villa that was built in 1896. She and husband Rob have lived here for 20 years and now share it with their children Anna, Imogen, and Theo—and let's not forget their dog, Ted. Oh, Ted.

From the kitchen window bench surrounded by potted and hanging greenery to the large fiddle-leaf fig (*Ficus lyrata*) that poses next to the dining room table, Dee's kitchen just shines with life. Dee thinks they have about 46 plants and I'm almost sure half of them are in this part of the house. While the plants beg for my attention first—I mean the plants and Ted (he was really into me)—the next thing that makes you feel settled in is how beautifully styled the space is. When I asked Dee to describe her style, she said, "I'm an interior designer and I tend to use my home to try out new paint or furniture styling ideas. I think this helps to keep my look fresh. My style is a mix of Scandinavian, vintage, and bohemian. I only allow things that I really love into the house. I think your home should be all about how you want to feel." Well, I definitely felt relaxed and at home in her space. Job well done, Dee.

If I'm being completely honest though, I think I tend to feel completely at home and relaxed in any home that has a lot of plants. It's just the feeling plants bring me. I'm sure you can all relate. Dee has always been into bringing plants indoors but explained that "It's gone into overdrive in the last four years. I love how plants are easily moveable and can instantly change the look of a room and add color and texture.

I think that the popularity of Instagram and Pinterest has opened my eyes to how many plants are available and how great they look en masse. Social media has made me braver about trying lots of creative things, including plants." I think social media is the driving force behind bringing the plant community together.

Dee recalls seeing plants in her grandparents' and parents' homes when she was growing up, and she has carried that with her into adulthood. For Dee, having plants around "makes me feel a lot closer to nature. I love to blur the boundaries between outside and inside, and houseplants are perfect for this." The decisions she makes for what types of plants to bring into her home are pretty standard, she says: "If I buy a new houseplant, it's normally because it's something I've not seen before. My most recent purchase was a philodendron, which I didn't like until recently. I now love the idea of growing it inside the house as a vine—which I first saw on Instagram." When it comes to where she'll place the plant once she gets them home, the way she decides is: "I think about the amount of light in that room. I also avoid radiators. I think about how the vignette of plants will work, and try and select plants of varying heights and with foliage that will both complement and contrast with their plant neighbors. I also think about how I want the room to feel. Some plants, asparagus ferns for instance, lend a lighter, delicate touch to a room. Others, such as fiddle-leaf figs, have a stronger look and give a room more structure."

GREEN MAKES A ROOM

Dee loves selecting plants of varying heights to give visual interest to simply decorated rooms. On the previous page, she has used a *Monstera deliciosa* and a Swedish ivy (*Plectranthus verticillatus*) to complement a large photo of Bob Dylan and a vintage leather chair, making for a great still life. Above, she has paired a tall marble column (*Euphorbia trigona*) on the left with a *Monstera adansonii* hanging on the right, above another Swedish ivy. In the entrance hall, a Boston fern (*Nephrolepis exaltata*) and Chinese money plant (*Pilea peperomioides*) are perfectly placed to catch the light coming through the door.

KITCHEN LIGHT

Dee's bright and sunny kitchen is where all the family hang out. With ideal conditions for many plants, nestled among the natural wood we can see (clockwise from the left): a philodendron, fiddle-leaf fig (*Ficus lyrata*), string of hearts (*Ceropegia woodii*), Swedish ivy (*Plectranthus verticillatus*), and a *Monstera deliciosa*.

While Dee makes sure that almost every room in her home gets a touch of green, she doesn't overdo it. You can see her putting this approach to use throughout her home. One of my favorite spots where this is evident is in her studio/office. Here, she limits the amount of greenery that comes in and selects plants which will mesh well with the mood of the room. On the opposite page you can see a beautiful still life Dee has created with a long string of hearts (*Ceropegia woodii*), vintage furniture, and feathery reeds and dried seedheads—this scene is a true picture of Dee's unique way of styling plants.

TED'S WINDOW SEAT
Opposite, Ted sits on his very own plant throne, among a satin pothos (*Scindapsus pictus* 'Argyraeus'), rabbit's foot fern (*Davallia solida* var.*fejeensis*), *Monstera adansonii*, and a heart-leaf philodendron (*Philodendron scandens*).

STUDIO SCENES

The softness of the hanging string of hearts (*Ceropegia woodii*) next to the Venetian plaster-style painted walls, and the small plants on top of the cabinet, really tell a story of how Dee puts together a room—every object is perfectly balanced and not too much.

WILD STYLE

HOME *Sara Toufali*
LOCATION *Los Angeles, California, USA*

Say "hi" to Sara Toufali—she's part of our plant-loving community. Social media has made the world so small and helped us feel connected to those that share the same passions, and this is how I was first introduced to Sara. Whether it is an image of her twirling in a summer dress or lounging in her home, what genuinely shines through is her happiness for life and love for what she does. So, I was excited to meet her IRL in her 1,000 ft² (93 m²) duplex cottage, nestled in the city of LA. She rents this space with her partner Edward and they share it with 90-plus plants—I told you she was a part of our plant-loving community. And that love is clear: Sara describes her style as "Bohemian, laid-back California style, with an emphasis on natural materials, neutral tones with pops of color," and she emphasizes it must have "lotsa plants"!

The vibes of a New Mexico landscape isn't a far-off description of Sara's style. Large hats and cattle skulls are a motif throughout, and a color palette of burnt sienna, terracotta, ivory, and shades of green creates the perfect blend as you move through. As a photographer, blogger, and interior decorator, what she does truly has an effect on how she creates her living space: "A few photos from my print shop are hanging in the house, and I love refreshing rooms each season, which I share on my blog. My favorite thing is sharing tips and tricks with fellow small-space renters on how to transform their homes and create their own cozy, green-filled oasis," says Sara. She and Edward moved in two years ago and, since then, have been bringing in more greenery: "We brought houseplants from our last apartment with us, but I was able to buy lots more thanks to the natural light and extra square footage in our new place. We have lots of windows, including in the bathroom, so I'm definitely taking advantage of all that yummy sunlight." One of my favorite mottos when it comes to styling a space with plants is, "Where there's light, there's green." I think Sara would second that.

When I asked her whether she grew up with plants in her home, she said, "Yes! I've been surrounded by plant-loving women my whole life, so that has definitely rubbed off on me. One of my mom's passions is working in her gardens and she's always had a lot of plants in the house. Same with my grandmother—she was always so happy to show us the new blooms in her gardens whenever we visited. Growing up, I was surrounded by forests, farms, and nature in upstate New York, so plants have always been a big part of my life." Here at home, that desire to surround herself with plants can still be seen. She says having them makes her feel more "happy, inspired, and relaxed." Where this is most revealing is in the living room, which Sara says is her favorite room in the house. But for me, the magic exists in her plant throne. Now, you know how much I love a good plant throne. Not just because they place you in a spot surrounded by plants, but because they create a designated space to just let your hair down and find your peace. Sara says that when her mother comes to visit, that's her go-to spot. After being there myself, I can't blame her.

Creating spaces like these in your home takes a bit of styling knowledge, but also an understanding of what types of plants work well in different types of light. When I asked Sara how she goes about bringing plants into her home she replied, "It's based on color, shape, maintenance, and lighting needs. Popularity doesn't really matter. It just needs to be a good fit for me and my home. I like to see where the empty spots are in a room and I fill those spots with plants that fit. I also always take into consideration what the lighting is like in each room, where the nearest windows are, and the type of plant that will be happy in a particular spot. You don't want to keep a cactus in a dark hallway, and you don't want a pothos sitting in direct sunlight all day." I love her thoughts here.

BOHO GREENERY
All the planters match Sara's style. From left to right: a fiddle-leaf fig (*Ficus lyrata*), bird of paradise (*Strelizia*), sword fern (*Polystichum munitum*), and golden pothos (*Epipremnum aureum*).

Sara's bit of advice for us was: "Do your research and pick plants that are right for you and your home. Don't buy based on looks alone. If you're a low-maintenance plant parent, you're going to want to get plants that don't need frequent waterings or upkeep (like a fiddle-leaf fig). You want to make sure your plants will be happy in your home, and that you'll be happy caring for them. The right plant is out there for you."

EVERY PLANT IN ITS RIGHT PLACE

Above left is Sara's plant throne, with a *Monstera deliciosa*. Above, ZZ plant (*Zamioculcas zamiifolia*) and a sword fern (*Polystichum munitum*) sit on the shelves. On the left are coral cactus (*Euphorbia lactea* 'Cristata') and orchid cactus (*Epiphyllum*). Opposite, golden pothos (*Epipremnum aureum*) and *Philodendron scandens* 'Brasil' hang behind a dining table, which holds an umbrella tree (*Schefflera arboricola*).

"I ALSO ALWAYS TAKE INTO
CONSIDERATION WHAT
THE LIGHTING IS LIKE IN
EACH ROOM, WHERE THE
NEAREST WINDOWS ARE,
AND THE TYPE OF PLANT
THAT WILL BE HAPPY IN
A PARTICULAR SPOT."

KITCHEN PLANT SHELF
A sunny spot for succulents like *Echeveria agavoides* 'Red Tip', and cacti such as *Parodia*, prickly pear (*Opuntia*), and golden rat tail (*Cleistocactus winteri*).

GOLDEN SHADES

Warm colors create a cozy, sunset vibe in Sara's bedroom. She has chosen a trailing heart-leaf philodendron (*Philodendron scanden*) which gives a delicate feeling to the room.

TRAILING VINES

Hanging creepers work in any room, but particularly the bathroom where floor space is at a premium. Heart-leaf philodendron (*Philodendron scandens*), satin pothos (*Scindapsus pictus* 'Argyraeus'), and air plants (*Tillandsia* species) all love humid conditions.

YOUR PLANT
JOURNEY

The road is long, and the path is covered in beautiful foliage. That's the way I want every journey to begin for me. For others, it seems like they've walked along a similar path. As you can see, so many of us are finding unique ways to introduce greenery into our homes. The homes featured here are just a part of the whole. While there's inspiration to pull from each of them, it took time for every person featured in these pages to find their own way through the brush, in order to land in a space that felt just right. These may have been lessons they were taught growing up, or developed later in life through dedication, trial and error, and hard work. Being able to understand your journey and how you got to where you are now will be better for the path you're paving for the future.

I'm sure there are so many people out there with similar journeys in greenery, and similar stories of how they have created spaces that are lush and alive. So, what has your journey been? How did you get to this moment in time with the plants you've brought into your home to love and care for? Are you a novice and want to create a space that feels similar to what you've seen here or others you've seen out there in the world? Are you unsure about which plants work best in different rooms, levels of light, or with particular care levels? Are you already on the path to developing a greener thumb, but searching for the next creative spark that will allow you to introduce more plants into your home? Regardless of where you are on your path, there are a few essential ideas that can help guide you in bringing plants into your home.

ROOM BY ROOM

THE RIGHT PLANTS FOR THE RIGHT ROOMS

If you're anything like me, one of your favorite activities is eating cereal as a midnight snack while watching reruns of Seinfeld, and you probably do this in your favorite room in your home. This is where you spend the majority of your time with family, catching up on the latest episodes of whatever is hot on TV at the moment, reading, playing with your pets, or just to find some relief from the stress of the day. Believe me, I know how important that is.

For me, none of the rooms in a home can be complete until they have a bit of greenery. Just a little touch of life in a room goes a long way—it can make a stale, dead space feel alive and vibrant. So, when bringing greenery into a room you want to give a bit of life, it's important to know which plants will thrive more when being placed in particular rooms.

When I first started thinking about which plants would work well in my home, I thought about how they live in their natural habitats. For instance, whenever I'm in a botanical garden or conservatory, I like to take note of the plants they have that I also have at home, and the atmosphere they create for them. In the tropical house the air is always humid and warm—there's the hiss of misters pumping out water vapor which floats throughout the greenhouse. So, I note all of that and make sure I place my tropical plants in rooms that don't get too dry, and I mist them from time to time. You'll notice that in a greenhouse, larger plants create canopies for smaller plants beneath them, which means they don't get much

direct light, so if you have the same plants at home, finding shady spots for them is important. That being said, I know there are also plants that can be styled more effectively in your own home based on the size, color, height, temperature, and foot traffic in a room. For instance, if you're looking to bring a plant into a room with high ceilings, I'd suggest opting for a larger plant or hanging a plant from the ceiling so that it pulls your eye up higher in the room, allowing the room to feel more full. If you're looking to bring plants into a small room, it would be the opposite. For a small space, smaller plants are key, and utilizing shelving to get them off the floor helps.

Also, let's not forget the health benefits a plant can bring—including cleaner air, more humidity, a greater sense of wellbeing, and much more—and what rooms they are best suited to so they can perform their magic.

Before any of this magic can happen, the first thing to look for is the amount of light that is coming into a room. You'll notice that I keep reminding you of the importance light has for the health of your plants. Let's say it together: light... is... everything. If I had a money tree for every time someone's asked me what plants thrive with little-to-no light, I'd have a house full of money trees, and nobody needs that. Find out which direction the windows face and you will know the quality of the light coming into that space, and this will help you determine which plants will work well in that environment. So, start there and then take it room by room.

ENTRYWAYS

First impressions can be hard. You never really get a second chance at showing your best self, so why not go all the way from the start. I think the same is important for the entryway of your home. When it comes to rolling out the red carpet, have a plant lead the way. But, not every plant is ideal for being on your welcoming committee. Entryway plants have to deal with changing temperatures that come with opening the front door, as well as constantly being brushed when visitors walk by. Here, I suggest sturdier green friends like snake plants (*Sansevieria trifasciata*) or rubber plants (*Ficus elastica*). Both of these plants have the ability to withstand heavy foot traffic and can also handle brief changes in temperature.

ABOVE AND LEFT Jamie and Drury do a great job of styling the entryway in their home. They have literally rolled out the red carpet and offered their guests a nice seat to take off their shoes, bookended with a snake plant to the right and a rubber plant next to the door. Again, keeping plants here is only possible if you have the right light. Their small couch is only 4 ft (1.2 m) away from the front door, making it possible for the snake plant to receive the medium to low light it needs.

PLANT Snake plant
(*Sansevieria trifasciata*)
LIGHT Bright indirect to low light
WATER Let the soil dry out completely
before watering. Water once every
three to four weeks

PLANT ZZ plant (*Zamioculcas
zamiifolia*)
LIGHT Bright indirect to low light
WATER Let the soil dry out completely
before watering. Water once every
three to four weeks

PLANT Corn plant (*Dracaena
fragrans* 'Massangeana')
LIGHT Bright indirect to dappled light
WATER Let the soil dry out completely
before watering

PLANT Rubber plant (*Ficus elastica*)
LIGHT Bright indirect to medium light
WATER When the top 2 in (5 cm) of
soil is completely dry

PLANT Dumb cane (*Dieffenbachia*)
LIGHT Bright indirect to medium light
WATER When the top 2 in (5 cm) of
soil is completely dry

ABOVE Wendy Lau has tucked a snake plant
(*Sansevieria trifasciata*) to the right of the front door
and placed a small *Dracaena* at the bottom of the staircase,
letting it be the first thing someone sees when they enter
her home. The frosted glass door and the window above
the staircase (not seen here) let in the indirect light that this
plant needs. Another nice thing about having a plant in your
entryway is that it helps you remember to water it. As they
say, "Out of sight, out of mind." Here, a plant is always in
sight, so always on your mind.

LIVING ROOMS

The perfect spot for plants in the home has always been the living room. I mean, how do you think it got the name "living room"? In most homes, this room is where you have the largest windows, which means the best light. So, it's here that you'll probably let your green thumb go wild and have the most plants. Also, in most homes, the living room is the first room you or your guests will enter, so creating a warm welcome is always, well... welcome. Making a good first impression starts with a good "statement plant." Let this plant set the tone of your room and, better yet, the home. For me, it's the room where I branch out the most—pun intended. You know how they say, "Go big or go home"? Well, I like to say, "Go big and go home, with a new plant friend"!

LEFT AND OPPOSITE At the Hunker House in Venice, California, a large rubber plant (*Ficus elastica*) sets the mood of the room. It has thick, waxy leaves, which can come in shades of deep violet or dark green—and if you're lucky you might be able to find yourself a variegated version with foliage in a mix of pink, cream, and green, making it the perfect "statement plant." One of the reasons I really love the rubber plant for a living room is because this is where most of the heavy foot traffic will be in your home. As its foliage is so durable, you won't have to worry much about damage to leaves that are extended into the room. In these images, you'll notice the light fixtures above the plants, and you might be asking yourself if they're grow lights, but they're not. These plants get light from the square window above and two large sunny windows to the right of the frame.

LEFT In the Barcelona apartment of Lucia Lopez, a medium-sized fiddle-leaf fig (*Ficus lyrata*) and an *Alocasia zebrina* soften the hard eges of the wooden wall in the background.

BELOW In the same apartment, Lucia Lopez has created a space so she can feel completely at peace. She has utilized the couch and plant setup not only to blur the line between indoors and outdoors, but also to create a soft line that separates the living room from the bedroom. Creating groupings like this is a great way to style a corner and pull a space out of the background, into the foreground. The dragon tree (*Dracaena draco*) that sits above the couch and the small fiddle-leaf fig (*Ficus lyrata*) on the floor are perfect for a living room. What I love about the dragon tree is that no matter where you place it in the home, it makes a statement. Its bushy, plume-like foliage reminds me of fireworks, especially how the leaves burst out of the ends of the thin branches. These plants need indirect light to thrive and, here, out of frame to the left, two large windows allow for this grouping of plants to get the light they require.

OPPOSITE In the Baltimore home of Megan Hipsley and Justin Temple, they are lucky enough to have beautiful crown molding, and it's also a real example of how, when there is enough light, a plant-lover will bring in all of the plants. Their "statement plant" could either be the large bird of paradise (*Strelitzia*) to the left, or the large *Monstera deliciosa* that sits as the centerpiece of the room. Either way, I'm here for all of it. What makes the silky, paddle-leaf-shaped bird of paradise the perfect fit for a living room is that its foliage tends to grow tall and long, placing it higher in the space, and out of the way, so you can live among plants without them being a burden. It also instantly gives off a tropical vibe and sets the tone. Here, it brings warmth and shape to a cold and linear space. While these east-facing windows are large, outside there are large trees and adjacent row homes. So, when the sun shines in, it's a mix of full sun and dappled light—combined to provide the perfect amount of illumination for the bird of paradise and *Monstera*.

RIGHT A really beautiful planter like this is a great way to turn a plant into a work of art. Here, a purple *Tradescantia zebrina* hangs high in the home of Justin and Megan, so that its leaves, which have a purple underside, can be appreciated.

BELOW LEFT Mike Puretz uses a Fabian aralia (*Polyscias* 'Fabian') and a Chinese evergreen (*Aglaonema*) to bookend some of his record collection.

BELOW *Monstera deliciosa* is one of the best plants for a living room. This tropical beauty has been one of the most popular indoor plants for the past few years, and I don't see that trend slowing down any time soon. Just like the bird of paradise (*Strelitzia*), a monstera makes a room feel like a getaway—think stay-cation all the way. While the bird of paradise enjoys the direct morning sun coming into this room, the *Monstera* loves the dappled light that dances along its foliage. Remember, think about how this climbing plant grows in nature: low to the ground or weaving its way around a tree.

ABOVE In Jamie Campbell and Drury Bynum's apartment, the shelves are the perfect home for a golden pothos (*Epipremnum aureum*), as these don't require direct light. A boxwood (*Buxus sempervirens*) sits on the coffee table, adding a pop of green.

PLANTS YOU SHOULD THINK ABOUT FOR YOUR LIVING ROOM

PLANT Fiddle-leaf fig (*Ficus lyrata*)
LIGHT Bright indirect light
WATER When the top 2 in (5 cm) of soil is completely dry

PLANT Rubber plant (*Ficus elastica*)
LIGHT Bright indirect to medium light
WATER When the top 2 in (5 cm) of soil is completely dry

PLANT Horsehead philodendron (*Philodendron bipinnatifidum*)
LIGHT Bright indirect to dappled light
WATER When the top 2 in (5 cm) of soil is completely dry

PLANT 'Marble queen' pothos (*Epipremnum aureum*)
LIGHT Bright indirect to low light
WATER When the top 2 in (5 cm) of soil is completely dry. Helpful hint: if the foliage is sturdy, don't water. If the foliage is limp, it's time for a drink

PLANT Council tree (*Ficus altissima*)
LIGHT Bright indirect light
WATER When the top 2 in (5 cm) of soil is completely dry

KITCHENS

I am often asked why I don't have plants in my kitchen or bathroom, and the answer is quite simple: I don't have any windows in those rooms. Honestly, I'm a bit envious of those that do, because they can be the perfect spaces for plants that like humidity and moist soil. Planting in the kitchen has its benefits, because when you're cooking, humidity is created, keeping the plants that love this type of environment thriving. It also helps that there is water close at hand, so when you have a plant in this room, you're often reminded to water it and doing so is fairly convenient.

ABOVE AND OPPOSITE In Baltimore, Maryland, Jamie Campbell and Drury Bynum have done a great job finding plants to help add a bit of life and color to their kitchen. With two northeast facing windows pushing light into the room for most of the day, they have many options for which plants to bring in. Here, they have some of my favorites for a kitchen. At the back of the kitchen counter where they store their cookbooks, a rattlesnake plant (*Calathea lancifolia*) brings a nice pop of color and shape. Calatheas are perfect for kitchens because of how often you need to water them. Keeping the soil evenly moist is key, so being near a sink is a plus. Because rattlesnakes can live in lower light situations, at the far back of the counter—away from the window—is a good spot for them. On the other side of the counter, closer to the window, is where they have their succulents. These make great plants for the kitchen because of how small they can be and how good they look grouped together in a row. If you did a survey on the location in a home most succulents end up living, it would definitely be the windowsill of a kitchen.

LEFT A large *Monstera deliciosa* makes for the ideal screen between the kitchen and living space in this apartment.

RIGHT, MIDDLE RIGHT, AND BELOW At her home in Toronto, Canada, Wendy Lau uses the windowsill and shelves in the kitchen to house her small plant babies. A boxwood tree (*Buxus sempervirens*) sits directly next to the sink, ready for the almost daily watering it needs to stay well maintained. The soil of a boxwood tree needs to stay evenly moist, so having it in a spot that reminds of you to water it is ideal. Wendy has even had a little fun planting a small combination of succulents in a tiny, brass bathtub planter. The kitchen is one of the most high-traffic areas of the home. When guests come over, it's the spot that brings everyone together, so having smaller plants here keeps the space from feeling cluttered, messy, and uninviting.

TOP AND ABOVE At her home in Dallas, Texas, Olive May uses a purple shamrock (*Oxalis triangularis*) to add a little life and color, and her silver inch plant (*Tradescantia zebrina*) trails down her kitchen shelf.

PLANTS YOU SHOULD THINK ABOUT FOR YOUR KITCHEN

PLANT Taro (*Colocasia esculenta*)
LIGHT Bright indirect light
WATER Keep the top of the soil evenly moist. Never let it dry out completely, but be careful not to overwater, and do not let the bottom roots become waterlogged

PLANT *Nephrolepis cordifolia* 'Lemon Buttons'
LIGHT Indirect to medium light
WATER Keep the top of the soil evenly moist. Never let it dry out completely. Mist weekly

PLANT Air plant (*Tillandsia*)
LIGHT Bright indirect to medium light
WATER Submerge in lukewarm water for five minutes, and turn air plant cup down to allow it to dry fully before placing back in its spot. Mist weekly

PLANT Jade plant (*Crassula ovata*)
LIGHT Full sun to bright indirect light
WATER When the top 2 in (5 cm) of soil is completely dry. Once winter hits, water less

PLANT Kangaroo fern (*Microsorum diversifolium*)
LIGHT Indirect to medium light
WATER Keep the top of the soil evenly moist. Never let it dry out completely. Mist weekly

BATHROOMS

When plants come to live in the bathroom, they benefit from the higher levels of humidity. If your bathroom has a window, any fern, *Calathea*, orchid, air plant (*Tillandsia*), *Tradescantia zebrina*, and many others would love it. These plants thrive in humid climates, and because hot showers are taken at least once a day in most homes, these plants will be living their best lives. Bearing in mind that this is also a place where people like their privacy, your windows are probably covered or have frosted glass, but no fear—these plants are also used to bright to low light situations. So, if its privacy you need, but you also want to have greenery in this room, try letting a sheer curtain filter light in, or use foliage to create a living curtain. A trailing *Maranta* or macho fern (*Nephrolepis biserrata* 'Macho') hanging in a bathroom window would do the trick. Just imagine how tranquil your bath sessions would become when surrounded by greenery. All you'd need would be a few candles, some essential oils, and you're living the art of self-care. Speaking of self-care, given that this is one of the rooms where we show off our birthday suits the most, you might want to stay away from bringing in cacti for obvious reasons—like the fact that they hold a thousand little knives—but also because they won't do well in the humid air.

ABOVE RIGHT Sofie and Yannick add a touch of green to their bathroom with a *Philodendron davidsonii*.

RIGHT Adelyn uses a ZZ plant (*Zamioculcas zamiifolia*) and air plant (*Tillandsia*) to add a little life to her low-light bathroom.

RIGHT At the Hunker House in Venice, California, the bathroom has a mix of all the perfect plants for this room. They have created a peaceful environment by placing plants in spots where they are effective in helping you feel like you're showering outdoors, but they have also thought about what will work well for the plant. Here, they have placed a sword fern (*Polystichum munitum*) along the path to the shower to add a touch of nature as you walk in and out. That small reminder of the outdoors will completely change the way you feel, pulling you away from the moment, and allowing that shower to wash the stress of the day away.

LEFT Also at the Hunker House, you'll find an air plant (*Tillandsia*) and a rattlesnake plant (*Calathea lancifolia*) enjoying the humidity and light in the bathroom. Air plants are perfect for a room like this because they love to draw moisture from the air, and having them there will remind you to dunk them in some water from time to time, which makes life so much easier for them and for you. Making your job easier when it comes to caring for plants is something you should always be looking to do. A side note: I love the addition of a timer in the shower, which will help you remember to conserve water. For us plant-lovers out there, being mindful of the planet we share is important, and trying to do your part to conserve water is appreciated.

LEFT AND BELOW In Wendy Lau's Toronto home, a green *Tradescantia zebrina* finds the perfect spot in the bathroom to hang out. As the shower is fixed in place and the stream of water falls straight down, the soil of the plant only picks up the moisture in the room, and does not get direct watering from the shower head. I love the idea of showering this close to a plant, but only if the pot is out of the way and does not take in water. You don't want to overwater your plant, so having a good sense of the moisture level of the soil goes a long way. Like I always say, using your finger and sticking it at least 1–2 in (2.5–5 cm) deep into the soil will help you know whether it's time to water. Across from the shower, Wendy has more moisture-loving plants: a creeping fig (*Ficus pumila*) and *Nephrolepis cordifolia* 'Lemon Buttons.'

PLANTS YOU SHOULD THINK ABOUT FOR YOUR BATHROOM

PLANT Rattlesnake plant (*Calathea lancifolia*)
LIGHT Medium to low light
WATER Keep the top of the soil evenly moist. Never let it dry out completely

PLANT Asparagus fern (*Asparagus setaceus*)
LIGHT Bright indirect to medium light
WATER Keep the top of the soil evenly moist. Never let it dry out completely

PLANT Air plant (*Tillandsia*)
LIGHT Bright indirect to medium light
WATER Submerge in lukewarm water for about five minutes, and turn air plant cup down to allow it to dry fully before placing back in its spot

PLANT Prayer plant (*Maranta leuconeura*)
LIGHT Bright indirect to medium light
WATER Keep the top of the soil evenly moist. Never let it dry out completely

PLANT *Stromanthe sanguinea* 'Triostar'
LIGHT Indirect to medium light
WATER Keep the top of the soil evenly moist. Never let it dry out completely

ABOVE I mentioned the rattlesnake plant (*Calathea lancifolia*) in the kitchen section, but I just can't get enough of this plant. Because I find comfort in being surrounded by greenery, I seek out plants for all the small nooks of my home, and the rattlesnake is one of the plants I try to sneak in whenever possible. They add a pop of color and live well in a low-light spot when needed. Like all *Calathea*, what's really special about them is the way their foliage dances around throughout the day—they lower their leaves during daylight hours to take in as much light as possible and raise them at night as if praying, hence their nickname: "prayer plant."

DINING ROOMS

If you happen to have read my first book, you are probably aware that what sparked my interest in the world of indoor greenery was my visit to Terrain, a nursery/plant shop in the city of Glen Mills, Pennsylvania. While dining in a greenhouse among what felt like hundreds of plants, I thought that this was what I would like every dining experience to be. Where a traditional dining room would have chandeliers hanging above tables, in Terrain they hung large staghorn ferns, and where room dividers would usually be made out of a solid material, here they had ivy tendrils draped like stage curtains. My mind was blown. I left that day forever changed. I knew I needed this in my home. But, at the time, I was sharing a small apartment with not much light, and I figured that once I had the light, the space, and the time to care for plants, then I would start to bring as many as I possibly could home with me.

Fast-forward eight years, I decided to transform my studio into the place where this all started... the dining room. The large windows and high ceilings make it easy to grow plants high and low; it's the care that goes into maintaining them that can be hard at times. For me, the idea of dining surrounded by greenery should be everyone's goal—it's the ideal version of indoor picnicking. While I can't say exactly which plants are ideal for a dining room, any plant could work based on the type of light and the type of space you have. Consider the light that is coming into the room and how you'd like to style it. Here, you'll notice I've lined the walls and windows with different-sized plants. Placing them around the perimeter of the room allows for space to move around the table. I completed the look by hanging a few high up in the room, in places where I can easily use a stool to water them.

Some might consider having plants in the same space where you eat unsanitary, but not me. Honestly,

ABOVE AND OPPOSITE In my studio, Jungle by the Falls, I utilize a bird of paradise (*Strelitzia*), a fiddle-leaf fig (*Ficus lyrata*), a few apple cactus (*Cereus repandus*) and hanging golden pothos (*Epipremnum aureum*), to create the tropical vibe I wanted to surround myself in.

I don't think many others would either. You might have noticed the shift that has happened in many public spaces and restaurants—you can even call it a trend. When I first visited Terrain back in 2011, there weren't many restaurants that were covered in plants. But now more spaces than ever before are filling their interiors with plants and creating more lush environments. I for one appreciate this shift, and hope that many more adopt the idea of blurring that line between indoors and outdoors.

THIS PAGE Bright indirect light floods into the space at Mike Puretz's apartment in Brooklyn, New York. The dining room is illuminated by a high wall of glass bricks at the top and a full wall of windows at the bottom, so the plant possibilities are immense. Mike is a prime example of a plant-lover self-aware enough to know his limitations regarding the time and care he can give his plants. Many of us would fill this dining room top to bottom with plants. I mean, if I had this kind of light, I'd take a leaf out of my inspiration board and create a staghorn fern chandelier like the ones I have seen at Terrain. For Mike, it is the perfect setting for his Guiana chestnut (*Pachira aquatica*), pothos, and croton plants. For these plants—and for almost all plants—morning sun and bright indirect light during the day is perfect. So, I can't blame Mike for doing what works for him. This room is incredible just as it is—and Mike is too busy hoarding records and books to overwhelm his place with plants.

PLANT Chinese money plant
(*Pilea peperomioides*)
LIGHT Bright indirect light
WATER When the top 2 in (5 cm)
of soil is completely dry

PLANT Guiana chestnut
(*Pachira aquatica*)
LIGHT Bright indirect to medium light
WATER When the top 2 in (5 cm) of
soil is completely dry

PLANT ZZ plant (*Zamioculcas
zamiifolia*)
LIGHT Bright indirect to low light
WATER Let the soil dry out completely
before watering, meaning you'll
probably water once every three
to four weeks

PLANT Golden pothos
(*Epipremnum aureum*)
LIGHT Bright indirect to low light
WATER When the top 2 in (5 cm) of
soil is completely dry. Helpful hint: if
the foliage is sturdy, don't water; if the
foliage is limp, it's time for a drink

PLANT Ponytail palm
(*Beaucarnea recurvata*)
LIGHT Bright indirect to medium light
WATER Let the soil dry out completely
before watering, meaning you'll
probably water once every three
to four weeks

ABOVE In Jamie and Drury's dining room in Baltimore,
Maryland, there is one extra seat for their Ethiopean fern
(*Asparagus aethiopicus*). With sheer curtains covering
the window behind it, this fern soaks up all the bright
indirect light it can. By maintaining a moist top layer of
soil, Jamie and Drury are able to provide the fern with
everything it needs. While I love that they have used a
vintage chair as a plant stand, Ethiopean ferns also look
great in a hanging planter.

BEDROOMS

I've never gone camping—I know, I know, that's crazy, right? Coming from Baltimore, camping wasn't something my family saw as a "thing." The closest I've ever come to camping was "glamping" with my wife in Big Sur, California. For those not in the know, glamping is glamour camping. Just a quick FYI: my wife thought it would be nice for us to rent a tent that had a queen bed in it, so that I would feel a bit more comfortable about sleeping outside. I'm not sure I'll ever feel comfortable sleeping outside, but the bed did help. While I didn't mind this situation, I honestly would have preferred to go camping in the "outdoor space" I created inside our home. You see, I have filled our home with plants so that I can literally bring the outdoors in. For me, my ideal way of camping is being at home among all the plants, ordering food, and watching everything Netflix has to offer. So, when it comes to bringing greenery into the bedroom, I tend to go wild. Given the right levels of light, a bedroom can be the perfect place for many different types of plants. Some plants even give off the perfect type of vibe for a bedroom space: snake plants (*Sansevieria trifasciata*), spider plants (*Chlorophytum comosum*), and peace lilies (*Spathiphyllum wallisii*) actually clean the air by filtering toxins and absorbing carbon monoxide while you sleep. While this might be on a small scale, I mean, come on now, every little bit helps. It's also beneficial that these three plants are easy to care for. If I'm honest, I do find it strange that some of the plants that are good to sleep near are named after animals and insects that you wouldn't want anywhere near your bed.

THIS PAGE In some cultures, I hear that it isn't considered wise to have plants in the bedroom because they are thought to prevent you from sleeping well, but I beg to differ. I have found that sleeping among greenery has only helped me get better quality sleep. We're talking all levels of REM. In all the homes in this book, you've seen bedrooms filled with plants, so it's obvious this isn't a niche idea. Many have found comfort in sleeping next to their plant friends.

BELOW When I set up the bedroom in my studio in Baltimore, Maryland, the first thing I did—before I put any furniture in the room—was to bring in a plant. I wanted a plant that would make a statement, and that plant was a fiddle-leaf fig (*Ficus lyrata*) I would later name "Treezus." The fiddle-leaf fig is perfect for the bedroom—any room, really—because it instantly challenges the idea of what an indoor space should be. In the perfect setting, a fiddle-leaf fig can grow up to 25 ft (7.5 m) in height, so if your bedroom has enough height, you can end up having a treehouse inside your actual house. Fiddle-leaf figs grow in a tree-like shape, so you won't just have a plant in your room, but an actual tree. This is the definition of camping, is it not? Every night, you are literally sleeping under or next to a tree. When it comes to caring for a fiddle-leaf fig—just like with all other plants—the right light is fundamental. The fiddle-leaf fig thrives in bright indirect light, so making sure that you place it in a room that has this type of light is key.

PLANT Fiddle-leaf fig (*Ficus lyrata*)
LIGHT Bright indirect light
WATER When the top 2 in (5 cm)
of soil is completely dry

PLANT Snake plant (*Sansevieria trifasciata*)
LIGHT Bright indirect to low light
WATER Let the soil dry out completely
before watering, meaning you'll
probably water once every three
to four weeks

PLANT Peace lily (*Spathiphyllum wallisii*)
LIGHT Bright indirect to medium light
WATER When the top 2 in (5 cm) of
soil is completely dry. Helpful hint:
when the leaves go limp, that's when
you should water it

PLANT Satin pothos (*Scindapsus pictus* 'Argyraeus')
LIGHT Bright indirect to low light
WATER When the top 2 in (5 cm) of
soil is completely dry. Helpful hint: if
the foliage is sturdy, don't water, if the
foliage is limp, it's time for a drink

PLANT Bird of paradise (*Strelitzia*)
LIGHT Bright indirect light
WATER When the top 2 in (5 cm) of
soil is completely dry

OPPOSITE AND THIS PAGE In Blake Pope's home, in Davidson, North Carolina, the bedroom plant game is next level. Blake does a beautiful job styling the green of the plants against the coral-colored walls, mixing different types and sizes of plants to make the room feel lush and inviting. Here, it's obvious that his "statement plant" is the large bird of paradise (*Strelitzia*). This beautiful tropical plant demands your full attention as you enter the room. Not only does it set the tone with its size, the fact that this plant is found in tropical destinations makes for a relaxed sleeping experience. To the left of the bird of paradise, Blake has placed the bedroom favorite, the snake plant (*Sansevieria trifasciata*)—which helps clean the air. Above the bed, a large window covered with screen filters lets in the bright indirect light that these plants need. What I love about Blake's setup here is that while there are many plants in the room, it doesn't seem overwhelming. If you sit back and imagine this room without the plants the spirit of the room would also be stripped away.

WORK SPACES

Now, I know you're probably reading this book because you have the day off or a bit of time away from work. Maybe you're taking the day to get inspired, and trying to find some creative ways to introduce a new plant friend into your home, or you want care tips on a plant you're having trouble with—but bear with me because I do want to talk about work. Not about you missing a deadline, but about how to bring greenery into the office. Whether you work from home or in an office, adding plants to that space really can help you get through the day. There have been studies done on the benefits plants have in the workplace. They lower people's stress levels, so they allow room to be more creative. So, you're adding a new plant, becoming less stressed, and cooking up fresh ideas at the office. That's a win-win-win. I think you deserve a raise for that. Since we're all hoping not to spend too much time in our workplaces, you'll need to choose plants that will be fine on their own when you're not there in the evenings and weekends. If you're on vacation, that's another story—you'll have to ask your coworkers to tend to your plant friends while you're away.

ABOVE AND OPPOSITE Blake Pope has the right idea for the perfect office plants, and has a large Peruvian apple cactus (*Cereus repandus*), a few air plants (*Tillandsia* species), and a golden pothos (*Epipremnum aureum*). These are all great plants to have in your workspace, especially if it's not in your home, because they don't require much attention, and you'll feel so much better knowing they're doing fine while you're away. As I've mentioned before, the plants you bring in will be based on the light you get in your space. Blake's work desk is next to a large west-facing window, which lets in a good amount of light during the second half of the day. If you work in an office with no windows but you really want to bring plants in, you're going to need a grow lamp that you can put on your desk. In my opinion, the cool kids at the office have always been those that have had plants at their desks, so there.

LEFT A trailing plant such as this golden pothos (*Epipremnum aureum*) is perfect on an out-of-the-way ledge.

THIS PAGE In Sofie and Yannick's home office, they have plants that require more attention because, well, they're at home. If a plant needs watering during the weekend, they're there to give it a drink. They have a few thirsty but amazingly gorgeous plants on their desk, as well as a prayer plant (*Maranta leuconeura*), an *Alocasia*, and a *Calathea warscewiczii* in pots on the floor next to the desk. Their desk has shelves hung above it, so they're able to place multiple small plants there. They also use small bowls to hold an air plant (*Tillandsia*) or two.

PLANT Snake plant
(*Sansevieria trifasciata*)
LIGHT Bright indirect to low light
WATER Let the soil dry out completely
before watering, meaning you'll
probably water once every three
to four weeks

PLANT ZZ plant (*Zamioculcas
zamiifolia*)
LIGHT Bright indirect to low light
WATER Let the soil dry out completely
before watering, meaning you'll
probably water once every three
to four weeks

PLANT Peruvian apple cactus
(*Cereus repandus*)
LIGHT Bright indirect to direct light
WATER Let the soil dry out completely
before watering, meaning you'll
probably water once every three to
four weeks

PLANT Rubber plant (*Ficus elastica*)
LIGHT Bright indirect to medium light
WATER When the top 2 in (5 cm) of
soil is completely dry

PLANT Air plant (*Tillandsia*)
LIGHT Bright indirect to medium light
WATER Submerge in lukewarm water
for about five minutes, and turn air
plant cup down to allow it to dry fully
before placing back in its spot

ABOVE In Sara Toufali's home office, low light-loving plants
such as the cylindrical snake plant (*Sansevieria trifasciata*) on
the left and variegated rubber tree (*Ficus elastica 'Doescheri'*)
on the right are tucked into little spaces. A terrarium, as seen on
the far right, is perfect for a desk, as they tend to be small, and
I could not imagine anything more inspiring than peering into
a self-contained green world when you need a break from work.

PETS VS PLANTS

KEEPING EVERYONE
SAFE AND HAPPY

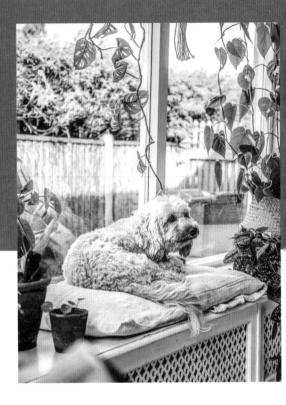

So many people ask about the pet-friendly plants out there, but where are all the plant-friendly pets? I mean, don't get me wrong, I'll take a good cuddle with a pup any day of the week, but shouldn't they respect all the other life in the home? My wife and I actually lucked out and have pets that don't care much about plants. Our cats Isabella and Zoey and our pup, Charlie, prefer the warmth of our home to living on the streets, which would probably be the case if they messed with the plants. I kid, I kid. But really... stay away from the plants. While I haven't always been a cat person, my wife's love for them slowly nudged them into my favor. I should note that the fact they don't mess with our plants really does help.

In my past, having plants and pets hasn't always been harmonious. I once lived with a cat that was what I'd call a plant terrorist. He expressed his hate—or maybe it was his love—by chewing on every single plant in his path. As most of the plants I had were toxic to him, I had to learn to help both him and the plants by placing the plants higher in the room, away from his little claws. I found trailing plants that could be hung useful for this, like philodendrons, Christmas cacti, and calatheas. Another solution is to grow larger tree-like plants that have tall trunks which keeps the foliage out of reach. Another good technique is to arrange plants on a windowsill, filling it up completely. This will deter your cats from jumping onto the windowsill—when they can't see a safe place to jump onto, they avoid it altogether. Lastly, if you see your pets interacting with your plants in a way that you don't like, this is the perfect time to pull their attention away from the plants by playing with them. In most situations, they play with or eat your plants because they're bored.

With our pets, they treat our home like they're in a real jungle. You can find our cats hiding behind plants to avoid our pup; sometimes they even flip the script and become the predator, peering behind leaves and jumping out at each other. The one thing I do know is that having animals in our home really does help with the "indoor jungle" vibe. While we might not have issues with our pets and our plants, I'm sure many do.

CLOCKWISE FROM ABOVE Dee Campling's dog Ted, the author's dog Charlie, and Alina Fassakhova's cat Usha.

FAR RIGHT Eryn Irwin uses hanging planters to keep her golden pothos (*Epipremnum aureum*) and finger tree (*Euphorbia tirucalli*) away from her kitty.

IF YOU'RE LOOKING FOR NON-TOXIC PLANTS FOR YOUR FURRY FRIENDS, TRY THESE LUCKY SEVEN:

1. Air plant (*Tillandsia*)
2. Parlor palm (*Chamaedorea elegans*)
3. Rattlesnake plant (*Calathea lancifolia*)
4. *Calathea orbifolia*
5. Chinese money plant (*Pilea peperomioides*)
6. Christmas cactus (*Schlumbergera*)
7. Ponytail palm (*Beaucarnea recurvata*)

GONE, BUT NOT FORGOTTEN

THE FADED BEAUTY OF DRIED FOLIAGE

They say beauty is in the eye of the beholder. I believe that to be true. What's beautiful to you might not turn me on, and vice versa. In the plant world, we pride ourselves on keeping our plants healthy and vibrant, and once a leaf goes limp, it's removed, and what was once life becomes trash. Recently, this has been changing. Many people are beginning to see the beauty in the dead leaves, flowers, and fronds that were once brimming with color and are now muted and dry. In their death, they have been somewhat reborn and can be seen with fresh eyes. What would once have been considered trash is now treasured and worked into the home as decor. I've been using this idea a bit in my own home, which started because I didn't want to discard some dying king protea flowers I bought for Fiona, so I chose to dry them out instead. The once soft pink and white flowers, while always retaining their shape, were transformed into auburn and gray shades. Now, in death, they live once again and have taken on a new beauty for us and been incorporated into our home. When visiting other people's homes, I've noticed the subtle use of dried foliage woven into their decor and have realized this has always been a thing, which is now becoming more popular. Dried foliage and leaves work best displayed in a home as works of art, separate from the living foliage they share the space with. A dried palm frond curling out of a large vase can give an empty

ABOVE Some king protea flowers with sentimental value can live on.

OPPOSITE In the living room of my studio, I have displayed two palm fronds that I pulled from one of the oldest palm trees at Rawlings Conservatory. Placed on either side of a bookshelf, they help add a little texture to the walls.

corner new life, or a dying bouquet of flowers can be dried and placed in smaller vessels throughout the home, adding little pops of color and texture in rooms that don't have light. At the end of the day, while the life of these beauties might be gone, they won't soon be forgotten.

OPPOSITE In the Berlin home of Theodora Melnik is a dried bouquet on a shelf in her bedroom. The texture of the stucco walls helps to accent the richness of the bouquet. The variation of soft tones in the different flowers is a thing of beauty.

ABOVE Latisha Carlson uses a single palm frond in her home in Albuquerque, New Mexico as a pop of color against the jungle-patterned wallpaper —it's also the perfect complement to the rattan furniture around it.

RIGHT Blake Pope tucks small dried florals behind his mirror.

PLANT SHELFIE

PLANTS AS
ART OBJECTS

As you've seen in the previous pages, I've had the wonderful opportunity to visit some of the most amazing and stylish green homes out there. When I entered these spaces, I was blown away by how unique they were, how they handled bringing in different types and sizes of plants, and how they cared for them.

But, there were a few common themes throughout, and one theme in particular tied all the homes together. It was the idea of creating a space to position your plants higher up in the room, whether on a shelf or another surface—this way of styling is creating "plant shelfies." It's likely you are a part of the plant community, so I am almost positive you've seen

ABOVE AND OPPOSITE Lucía Lopez propagates her *Begonia maculata* among her photos and an old camera.

LEFT Marisa and Curro use this shelf to show off their love of texture and art, and splash in a little greenery by adding a ZZ plant (*Zamioculcas zamiifolia*) and spider plant (*Chlorophytum comosum*).

images of plant shelfies on social media. If you haven't, it's about finding cool ways to arrange plants on shelves, and it can be plants mixed with books, precious knickknacks, and treasures, or it can just be a complete shelf dedicated to celebrating greenery. What makes creating a shelf like this special is that it gives you the opportunity to display your plants like the works of art they are. Some people are so into the plant lifestyle that they've become real collectors, bringing in some rare finds. And when we're talking rare plants, we're talking expensive purchases, so having the ability to display them means you can focus on their care and distinguish them from your other plants so you can show off your collection.

In most cases, plant shelves are created with smaller varieties of plants. I mean, you might find it pretty difficult to place a large fan palm in the middle of your bookshelf. But hey, who am I to try to hamper your creativity? It's the smaller size of these plants that makes styling them on a bookshelf so interesting and cool, and it allows you to have a good number of plants displayed in one place.

There are added benefits to creating plant shelves, for one thing, you're able to raise your plants off the floor, keeping them out of the way of foot traffic. Another benefit is that if you have a charismatic cat or a problematic pup, placing your plants on shelves will keep them from getting into a bad situation and killing the plants or possibly harming themselves.

Plant-shelfie styling is one of the most creative ways to show off your individuality and passion for greenery. There are so many different types of small planters out there, including beautiful, handcrafted

OPPOSITE AND ABOVE In Paul Holt's office at N1 Garden Centre in London, these shelves are a dream for collectors, with a coppertone snake plant (*Sansevieria kirkii*), *Alocasia* 'Bambino' and *Anthurium pallidiflorum*.

ABOVE LEFT Alina Fassakhova uses a heart-leaf philodendron (*Philodendron scandens*), an *Anthurium pallidiflorum*, and her *Stephania erecta* to set the tone.

ceramic styles, so being able to find a variety and start a collection is just as much a way of exploring your passions as collecting vintage records, glassware, or art. Creating a space like this isn't something that I would call difficult, but I would say it does require being able to reach all of the plants on your shelf so that the care process is made easy and seamless. Don't make a job more difficult than it has to be. So, get out there and build your own plant shelf, because we're all waiting to see your next plant shelfie.

CREDITS

Hilton Carter
@hiltoncarter
thingsbyhc.com

INSPIRED
Barbican Conservatory
@barbicancentre
barbican.org.uk

Isabella Stewart Gardner Museum
@gardnermuseum
gardnermuseum.org

Rawlings Conservatory
@rawlingsconservatory
rawlingsconservatory.org

Royal Botanic Gardens
@kewgardens
kew.org

Garfield Park Conservatory
@gpconservatory
garfieldconservatory.org

JOURNEYS IN GREENERY
Alina Fassakhova
@alina.fassakhova
alinafassakhova.com

Dabito
@dabito
oldbrandnew.com

Theodora Melnik
@_____theo

Sofie Vertongen
and Yannick De Neef
@sof_e @ydeneef
@theplantcorner
theplantcorner.com

Jesse Maguire
@roomandroot
roomandroot.com

Adelyn Duchala
@adduchala
adelynduchalaphotography.com

Marissa McInturff
and Curro Bernabeu
@marimasot @currelas
marimasot.com

Latisha Carlson
@nolongerwander
nolongerwander.com

Joel Bernstein
cavendishstudios.com

Whitney Leigh Morris
and Adam Winkleman
@whitneyleighmorris
@adamwinkleman
tinycanalcottage.com

Dee Campling
@deecampling
dee-campling.com

Sara Toufali
@saratoufali
blackandblooms.com

YOUR PLANT JOURNEY
Wendy Lau
@thekwendyhome

Blake Pope
@mblakepope

Jamie Campbell and Drury Bynum
@shinecreativetv

Hunker
@hunkerhome

Olive May
@oliveinwanderland

Justin Timothy Temple
and Megan Hipsley
@justintimothytemple @m.e.hips

Lucia Lopez
@lucialucelucira

Mike Puretz
@thehangglider

Eryn Irwin
@leaves.and.bones

N1 Garden Centre
@n1gardencentre

INDEX

THANKS & LOVE

I'm so very thankful to have had the opportunity to create this book. While it was a lot of work, it was also the most fun I'd had working on a project in a really long time. With that being said, there's so many I'd like to thank:

First and foremost, I'd like to thank my wife, Fiona, because without her love, support, and patience, this book wouldn't have been possible. I love you deeply. I spent many days away from home traveling to capture the lives of others, and it was her daily words of love and encouragement that kept me going. Fiona, you're the flame that burns within me, continuously pushing me to be better, challenging me to go further. I thrive because of your care. Thank you.

To my loving family and close friends for keeping me grounded and supporting me throughout all of this—thank you.

To all of the wonderful individuals that invited me into their wild interiors so that I could capture a small moment in time and share it with everyone here: you all were so kind, open, generous with your time and space, and made me feel completely at home. The indoor jungles you've all created are awe-inspiring in their lushness and creativity, and I'm sure so many will walk away feeling as I did. I learned so much from seeing up-close how you've all worked greenery into your living spaces, and hearing how your journeys brought you to where you are and made you the plant-lovers you are today. I hope I captured the true essence of your spaces and did them justice. While not all of us got to spend a ton of time together in this process, we could all relate on so many levels. I left many of you feeling I'd made lifelong friends, and I hope I left the same impression with you. I look forward to our next visits and I wish you, your sweet pets, and the many plant friends you have continued growth and love. Thank you.

Thank you to the team at CICO Books for helping to create such a lovely book and allowing me to be

me throughout the process. To Cindy Richards, tha for taking a shot on me with my first book, *Wild a Home*, and here again, and thanks to Anna Galkin and Megan Smith for being such great collaborat You've all put so much time and energy into maki this book and I'll be forever grateful.

Lastly, a thanks to you, the green-loving community. It has been because of your continued support and the success of *Wild at Home* that this opportunity was created. During the past year, it has been such a pleasure getting to meet so many of you in person, and I look forward to meeting more of you in the future. I hope in reading this, you're able to relate in some way and pull a bit of inspiration and knowledge from this book to apply to the wild interiors you have at home. With that, keep dancing in the dappled light and always stay wild!

This book is dedicated to my mother Tracy and my goddaughter, Sienna. I love you.